Clearly Coloring's Nature's Glow

A Friendly All Ages Coloring Book
Of Animals, Birds, Fish and Flowers

Selected Illustrations from the previously published
"Inspired by Nature Volumes 1 and 2"

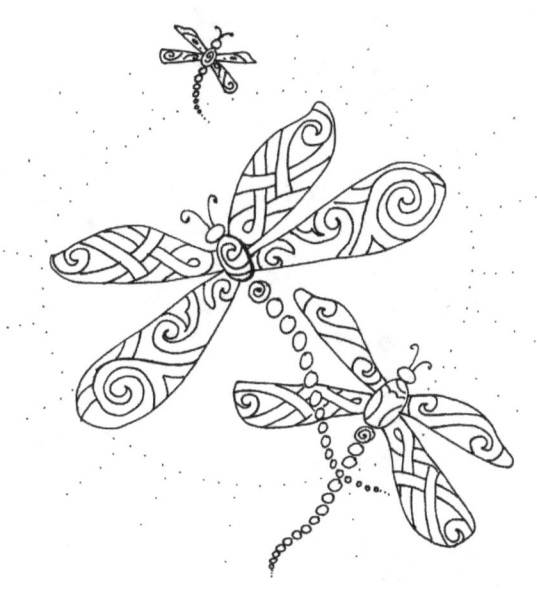

Compiled by Kristina Heth
Illustrated by Louise Bremer,
Kristina Heth, and Angelica Heth

Clearly Coloring's
Nature's Glow

A Friendly All Ages Coloring Book
Of Animals, Birds, Fish and Flowers

Selected Illustrations from the formerly published "Inspired

by Nature Volumes 1 and 2"

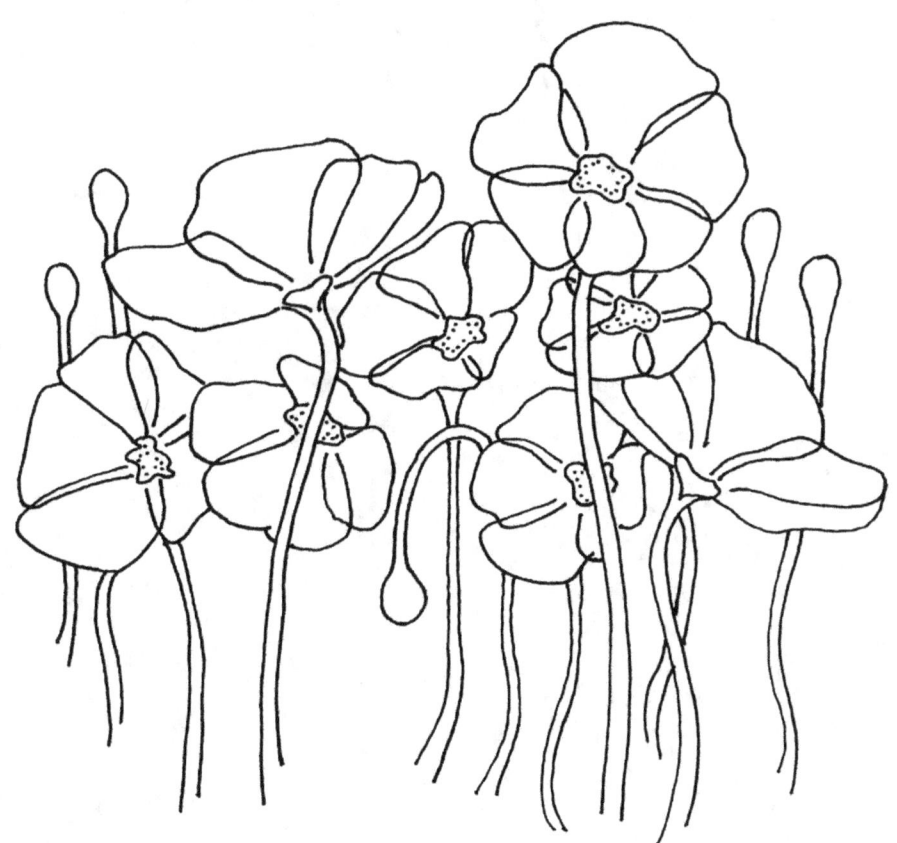

ISBN-13: 978-1542565240

Coloring...

Calms the mind-repetitive movement and a focus on simple tasks calm the mind and decreases stress.

Promotes attention-Focusing on coloring a space helps decrease distractions around us, and helps maintain focus on one task for longer.

Builds self-confidence-there are no wrong answers or wrong choices with coloring, and completing a space or page increases self-esteem.

Increases eye hand coordination-movement from your fingers sends a message to your brain, and builds up the pathways of this signal.

Boosts hand, finger, and arm strength-from grip strength, to muscle endurance, coloring rebuilds strength lost from injury or illness, accidents, aging, and reduced use.

Enhances creativity-coloring uses both sides of your brain and improves those parts of your brain working together.

Expands your vision-coloring is a fun way to relearn the ability to see when parts of your vision are lost following stroke, disease, or illness.

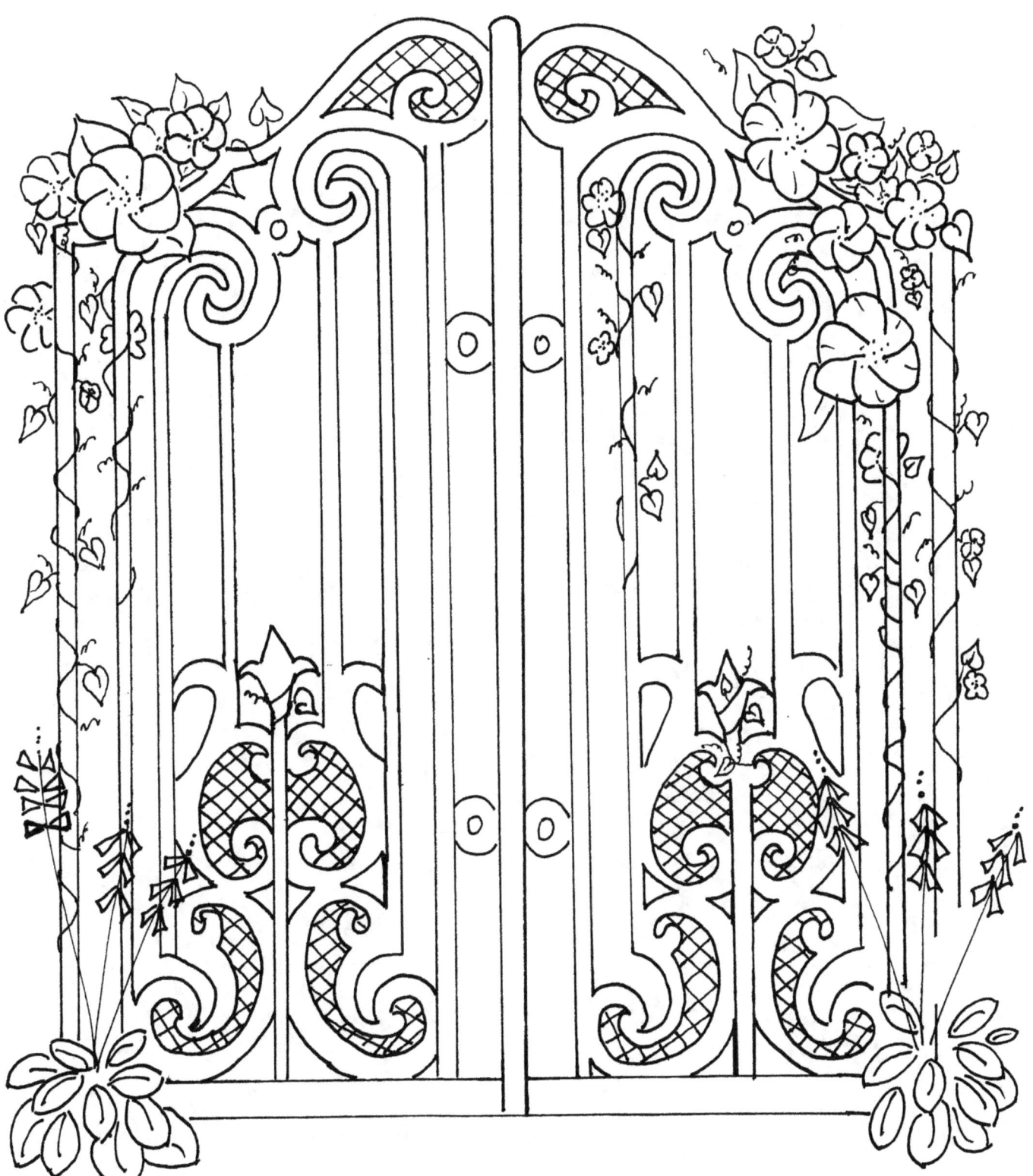

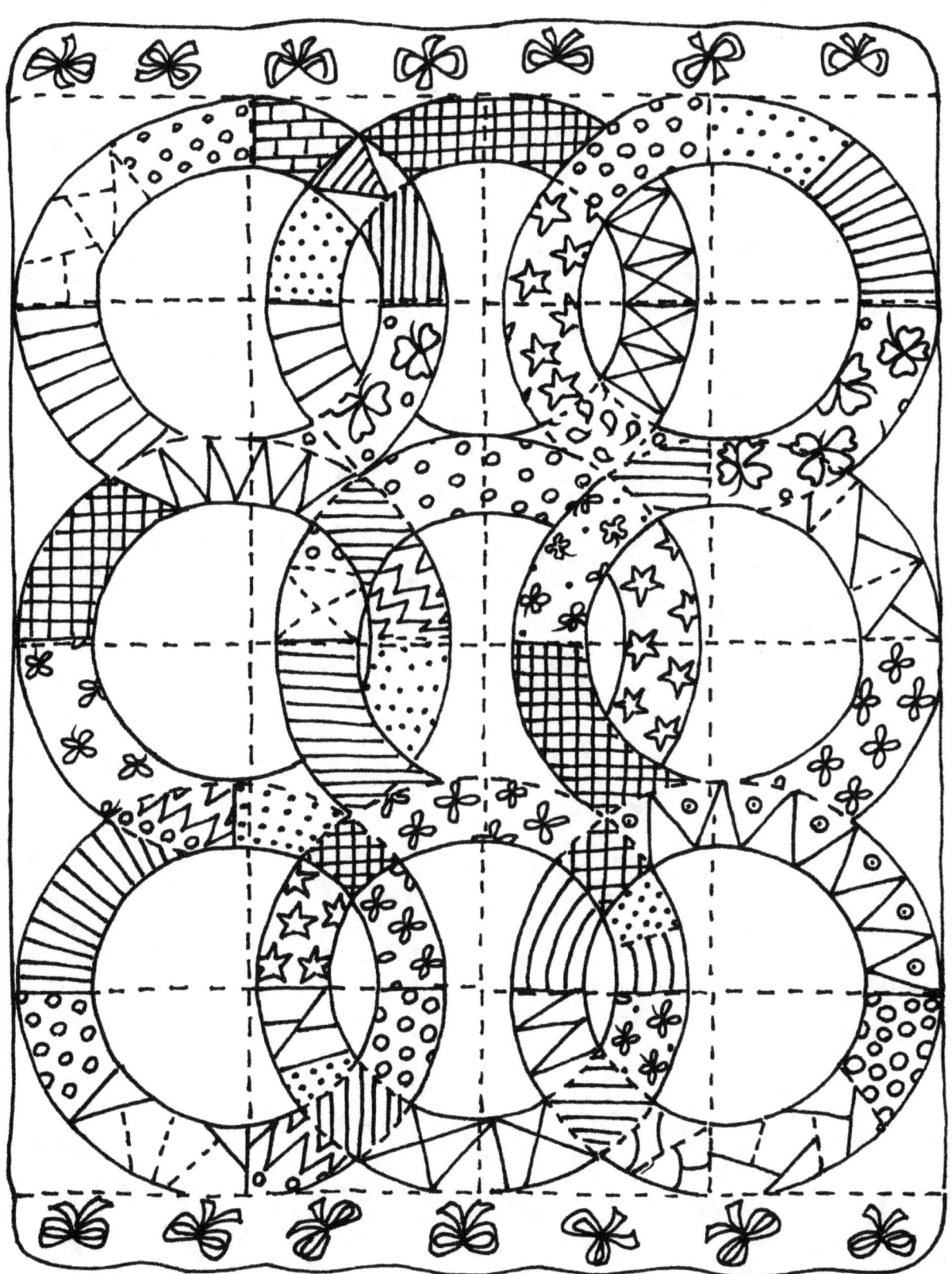

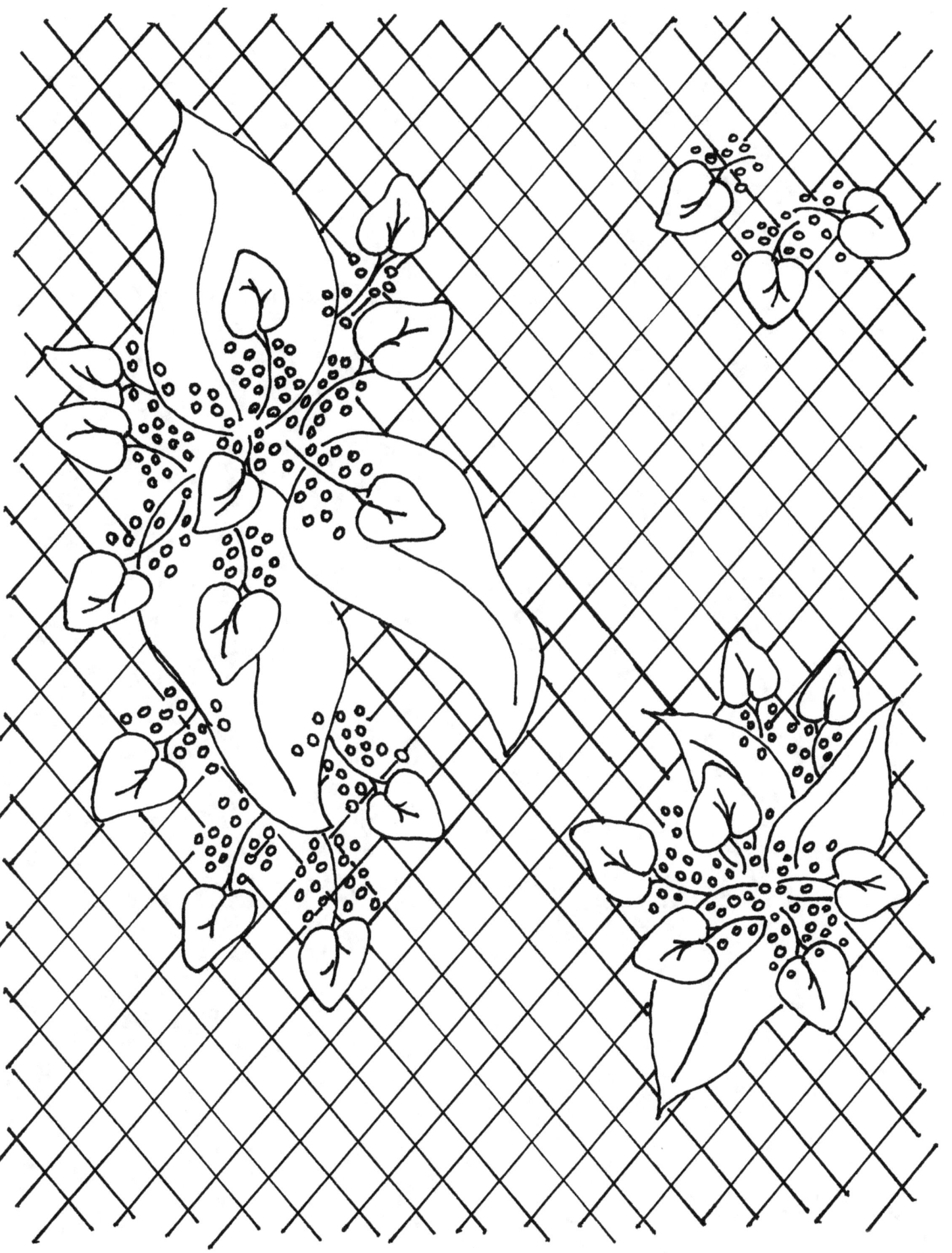

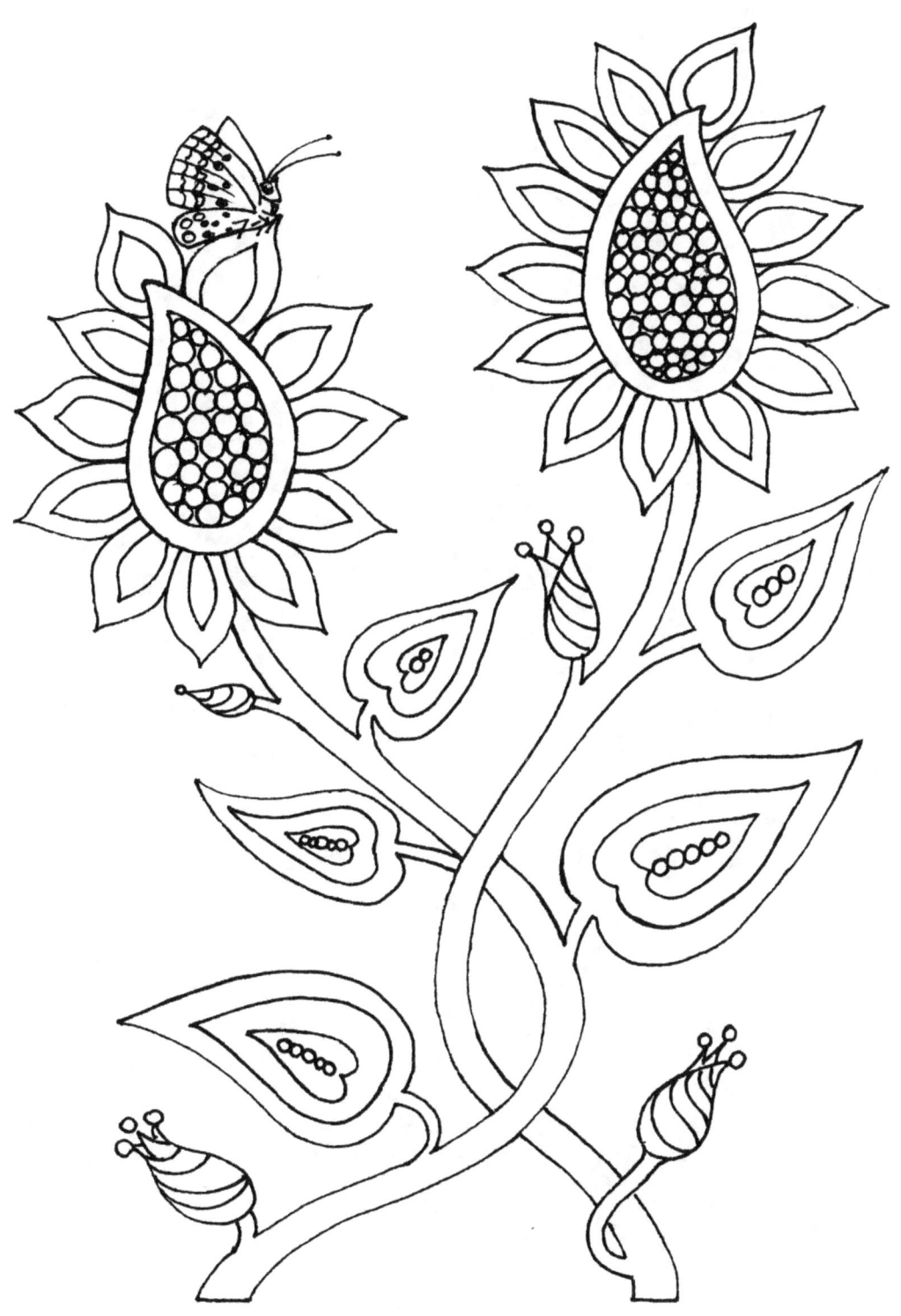

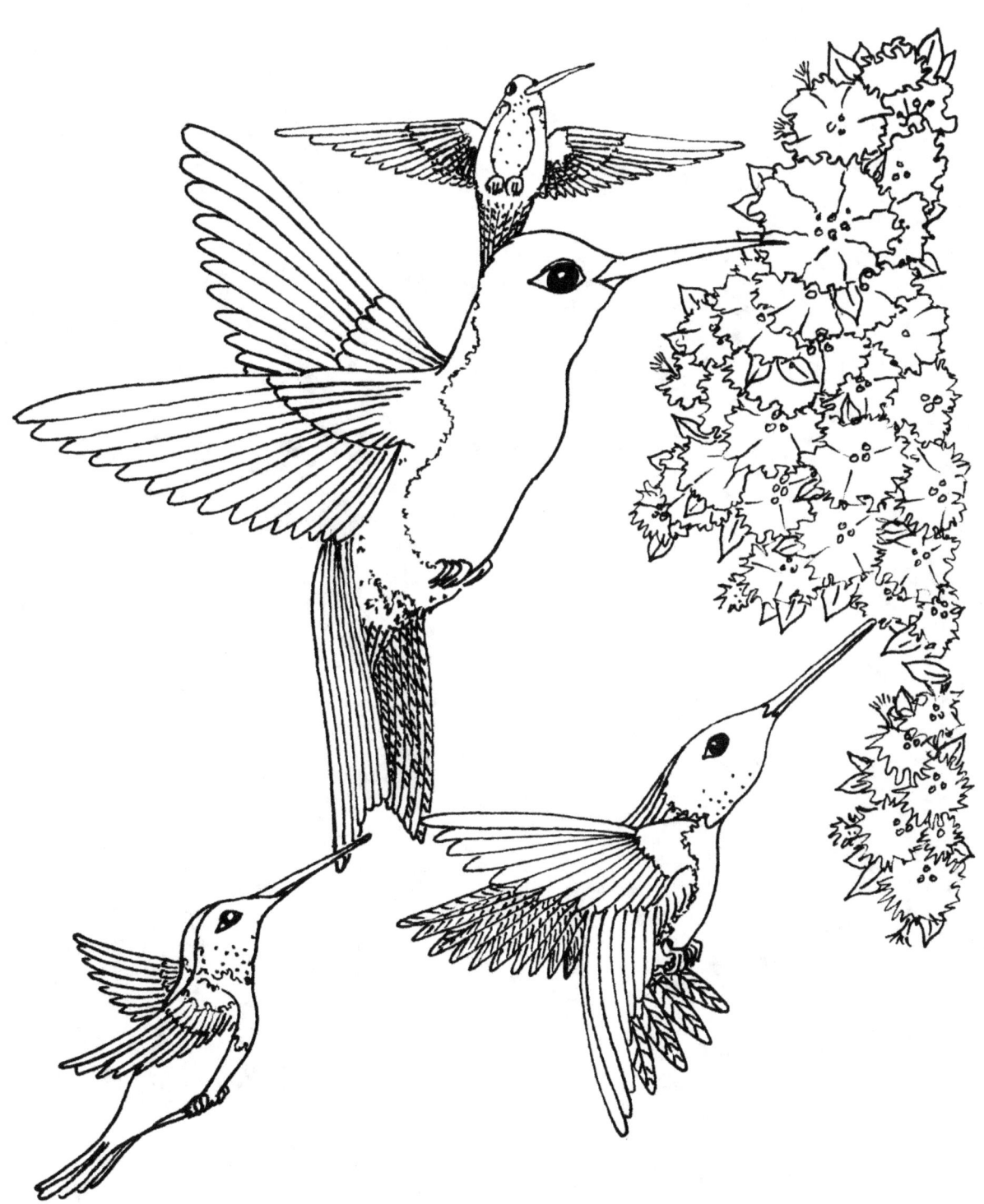

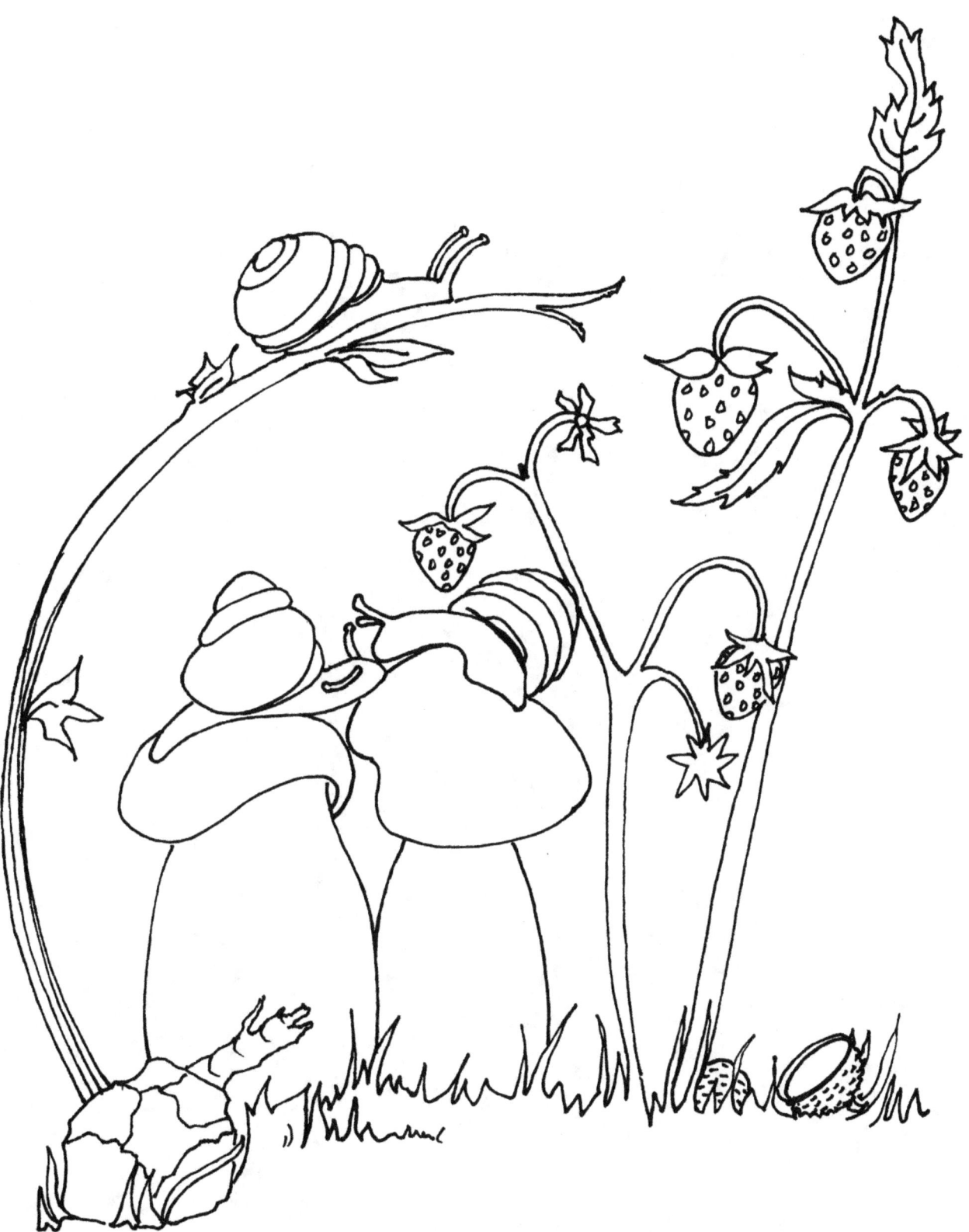

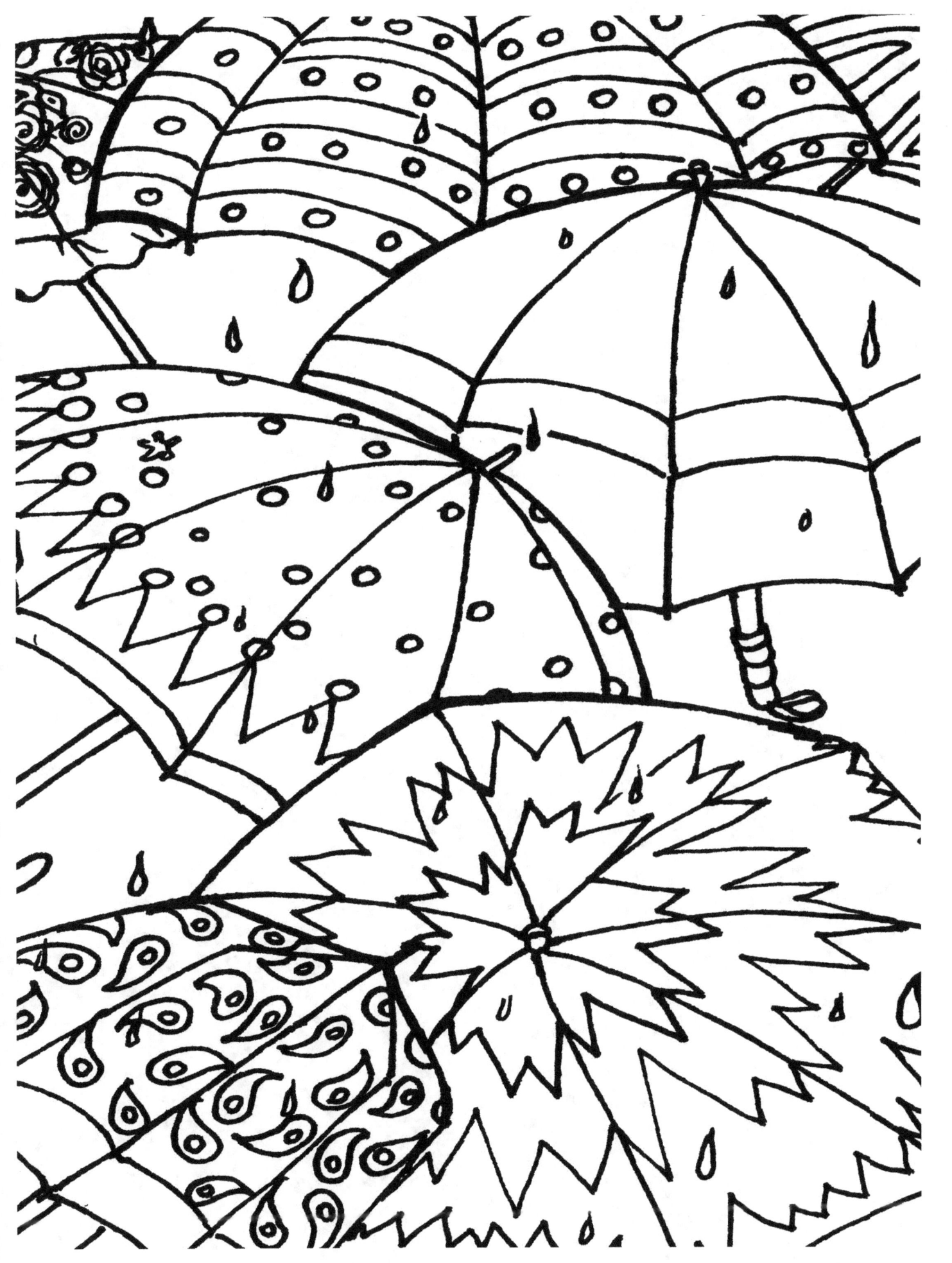

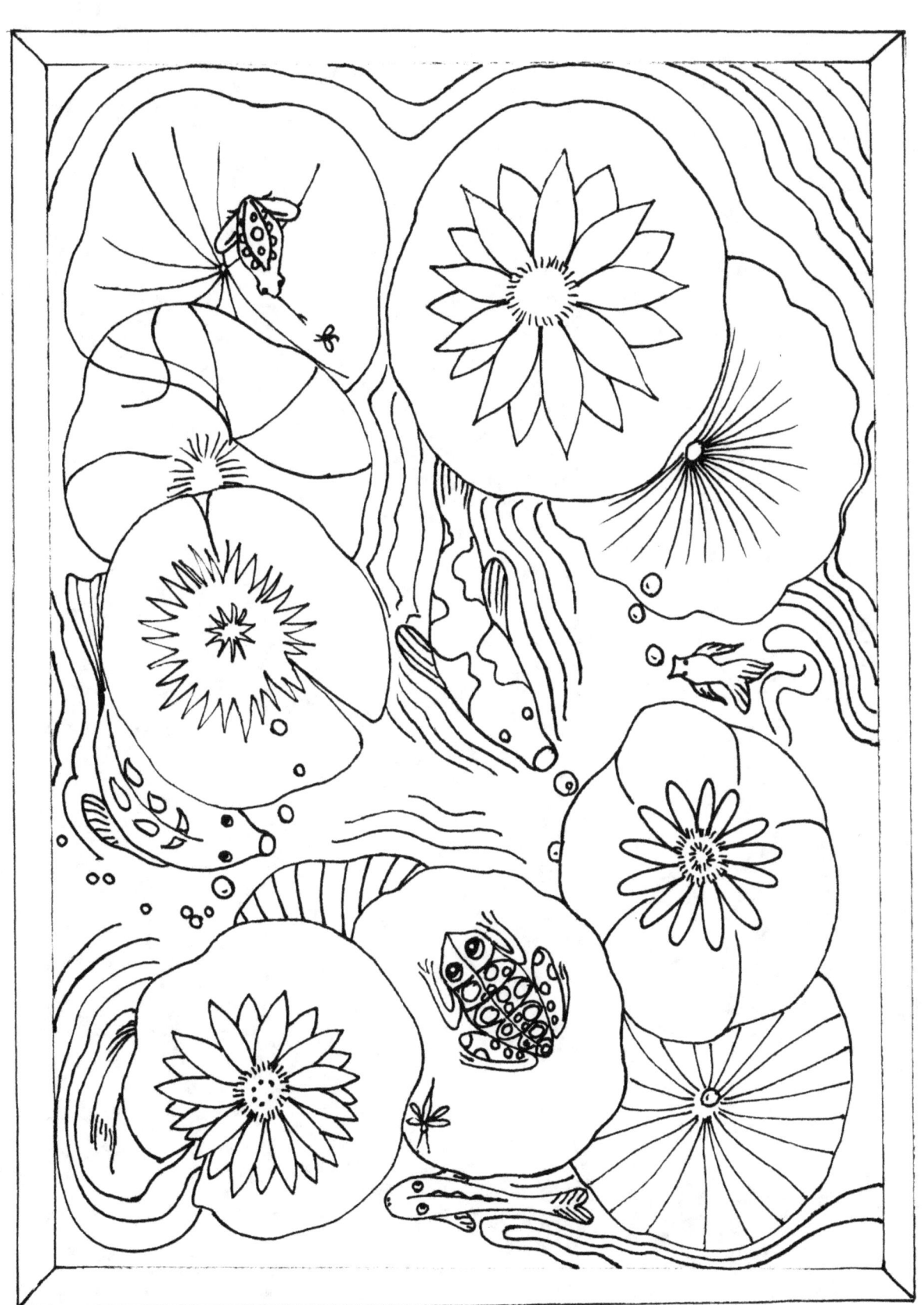

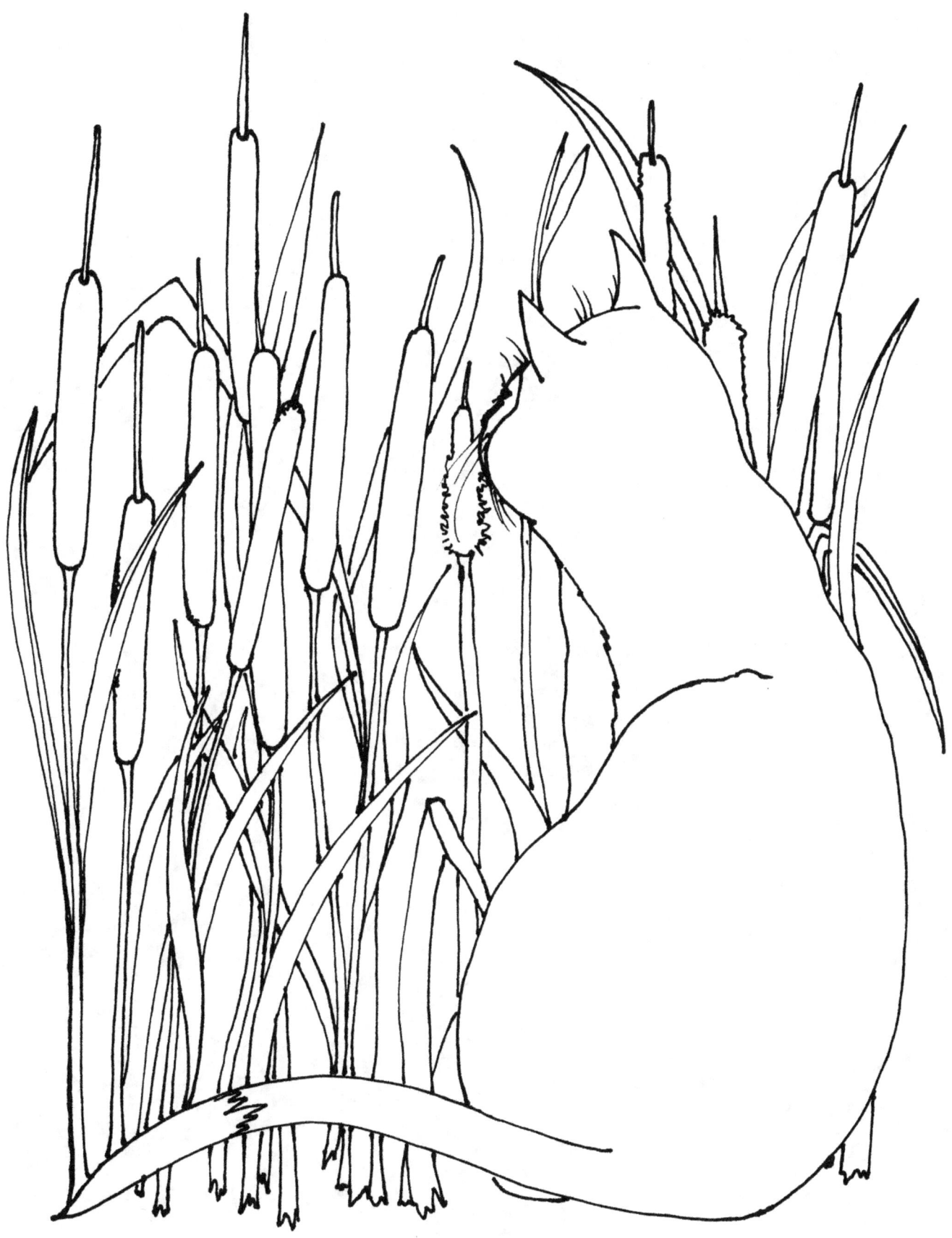

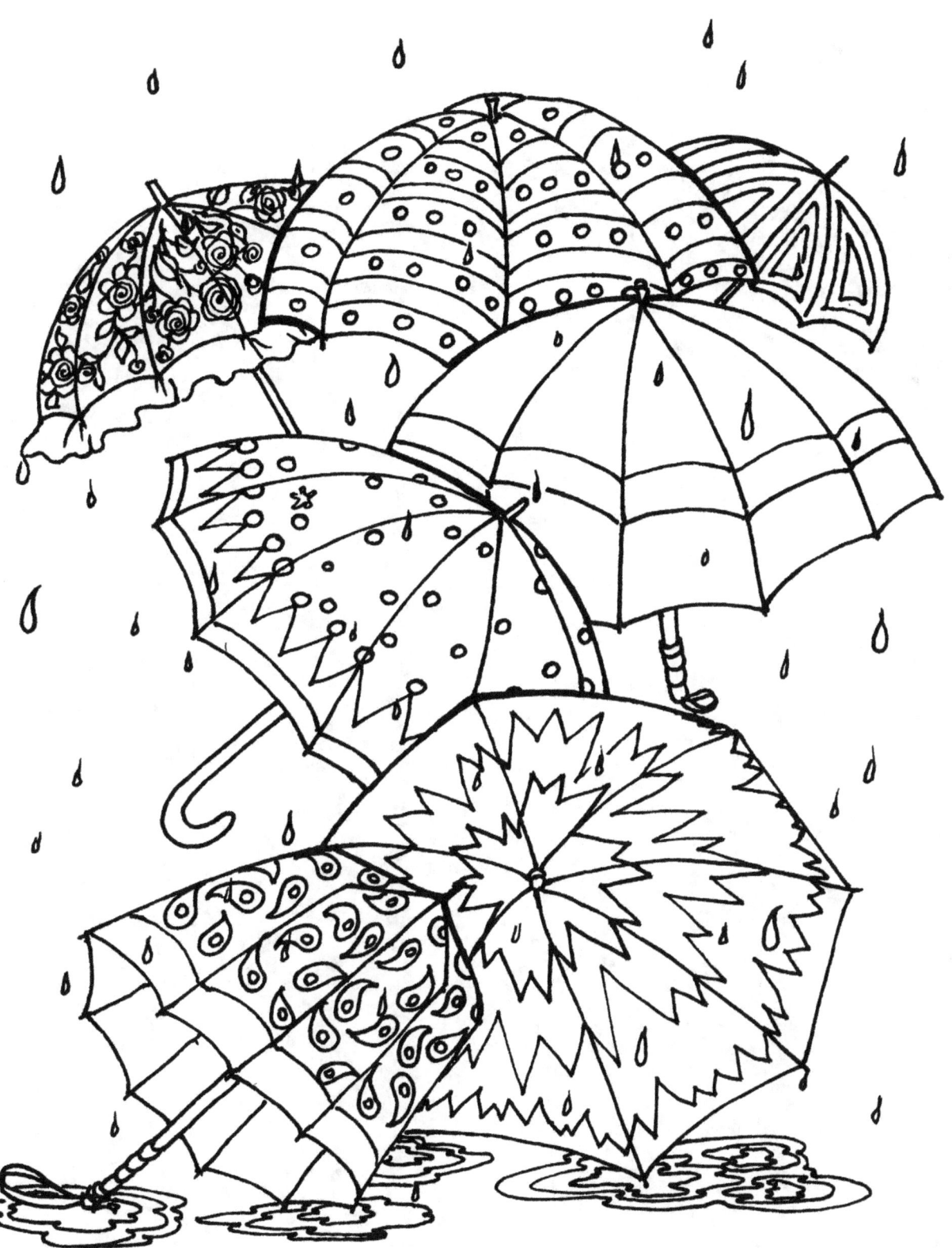

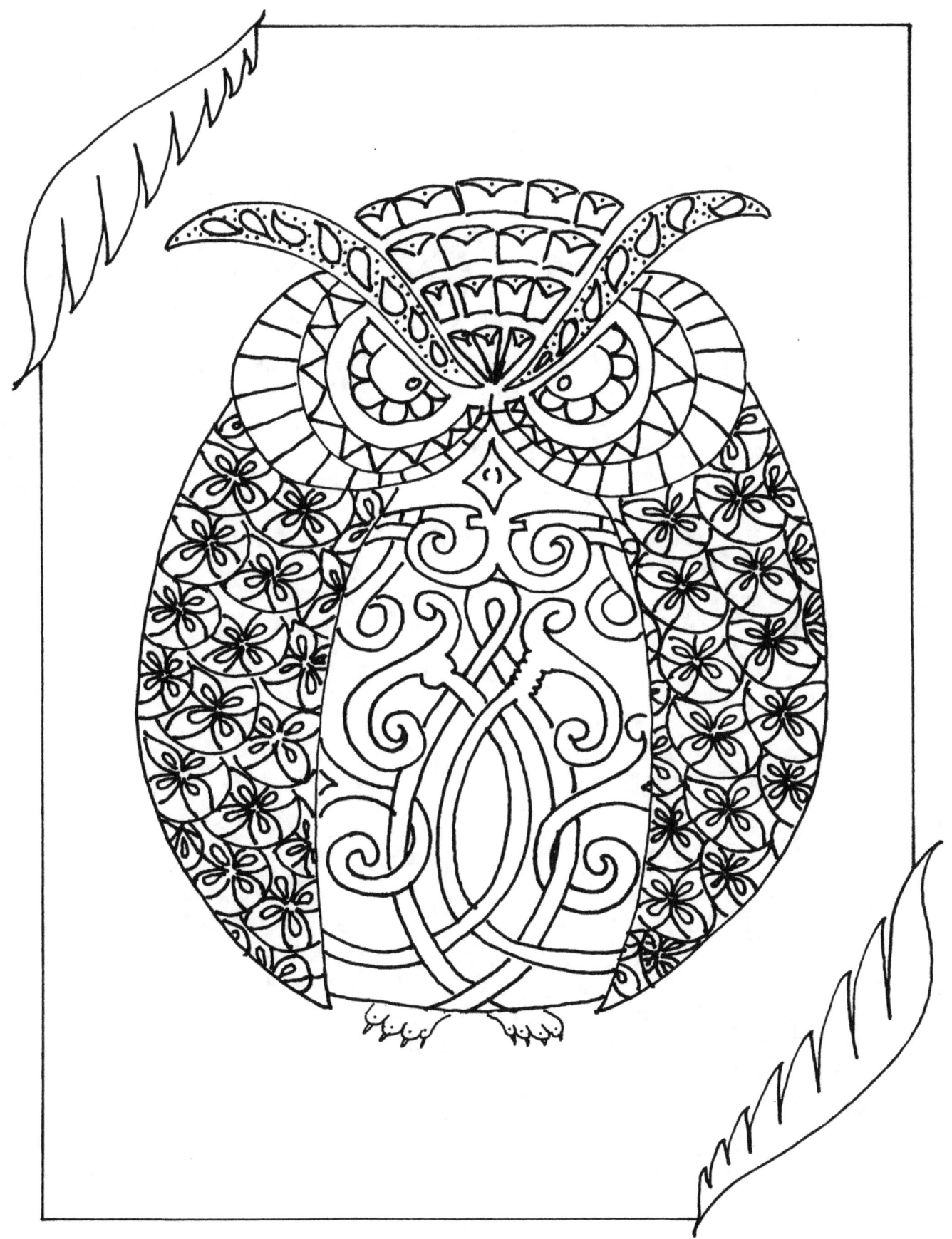

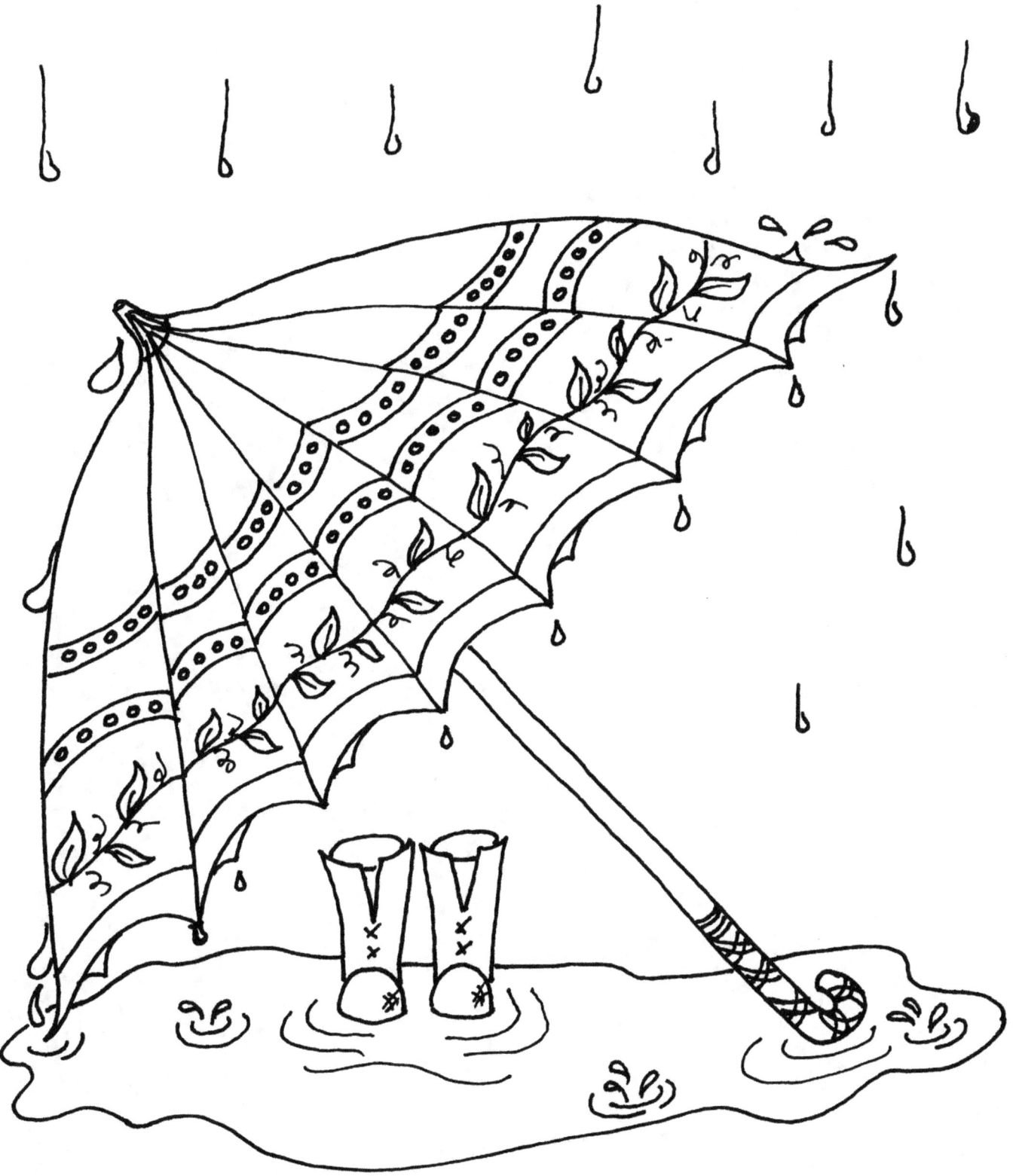

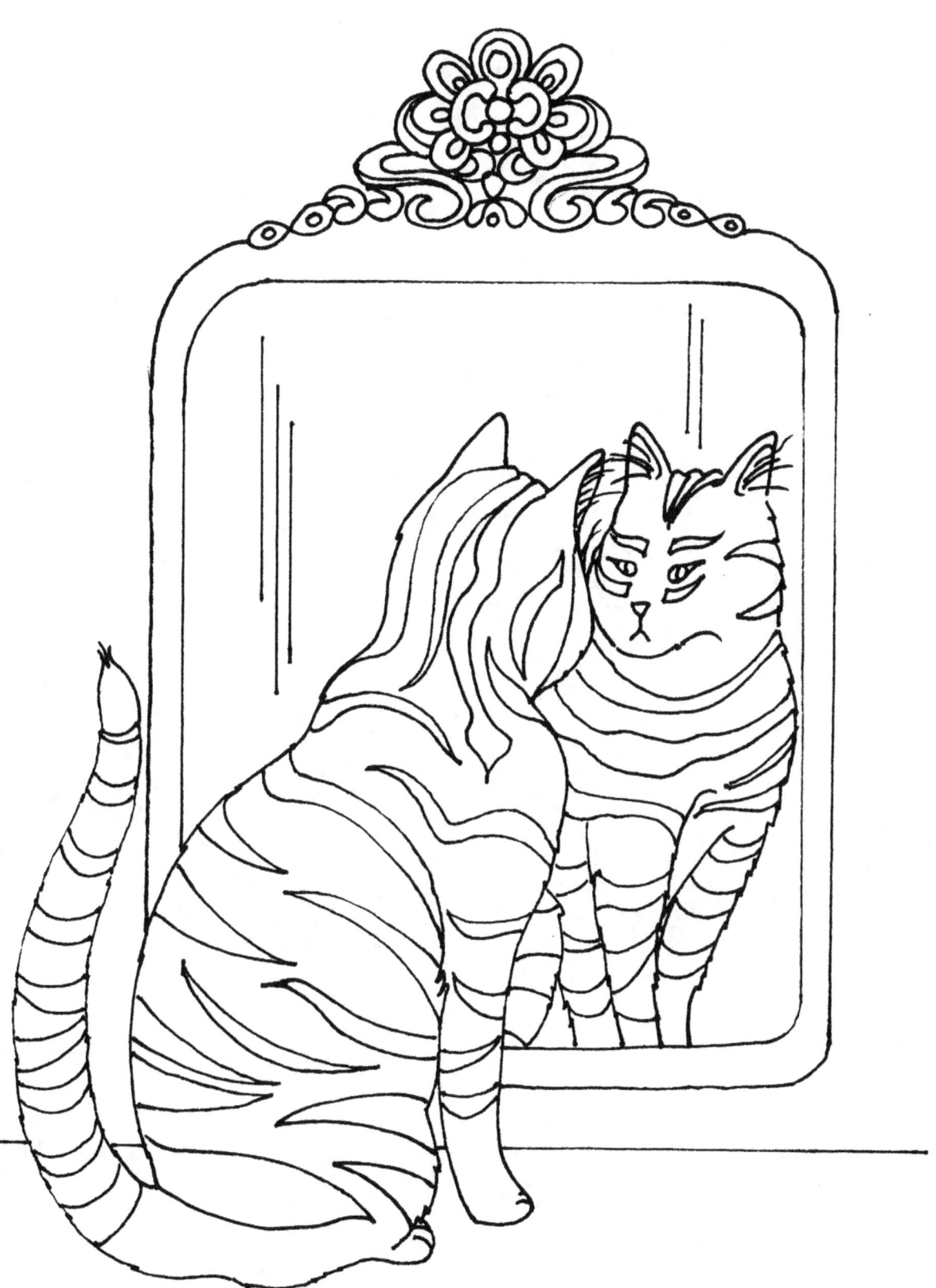

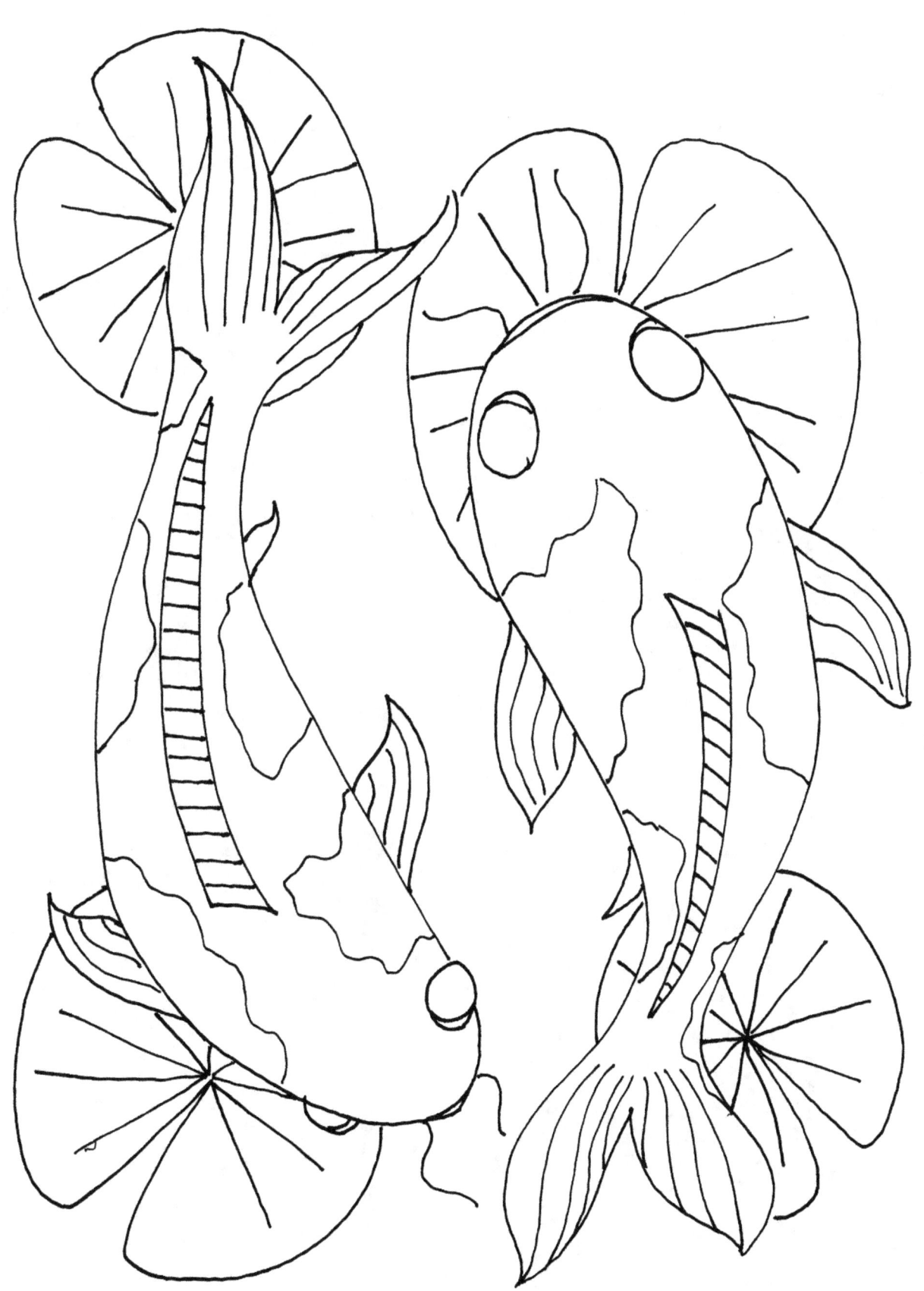

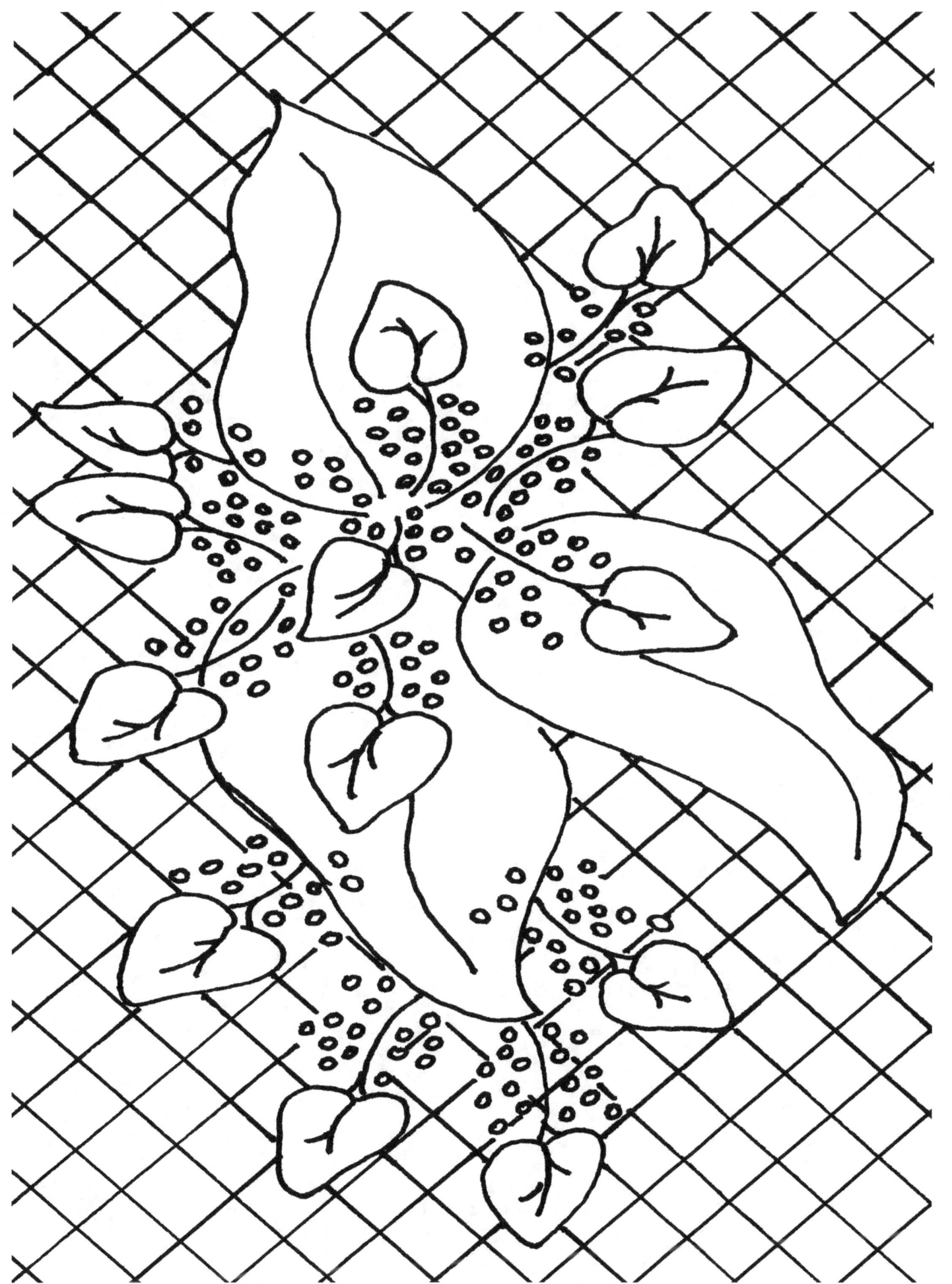

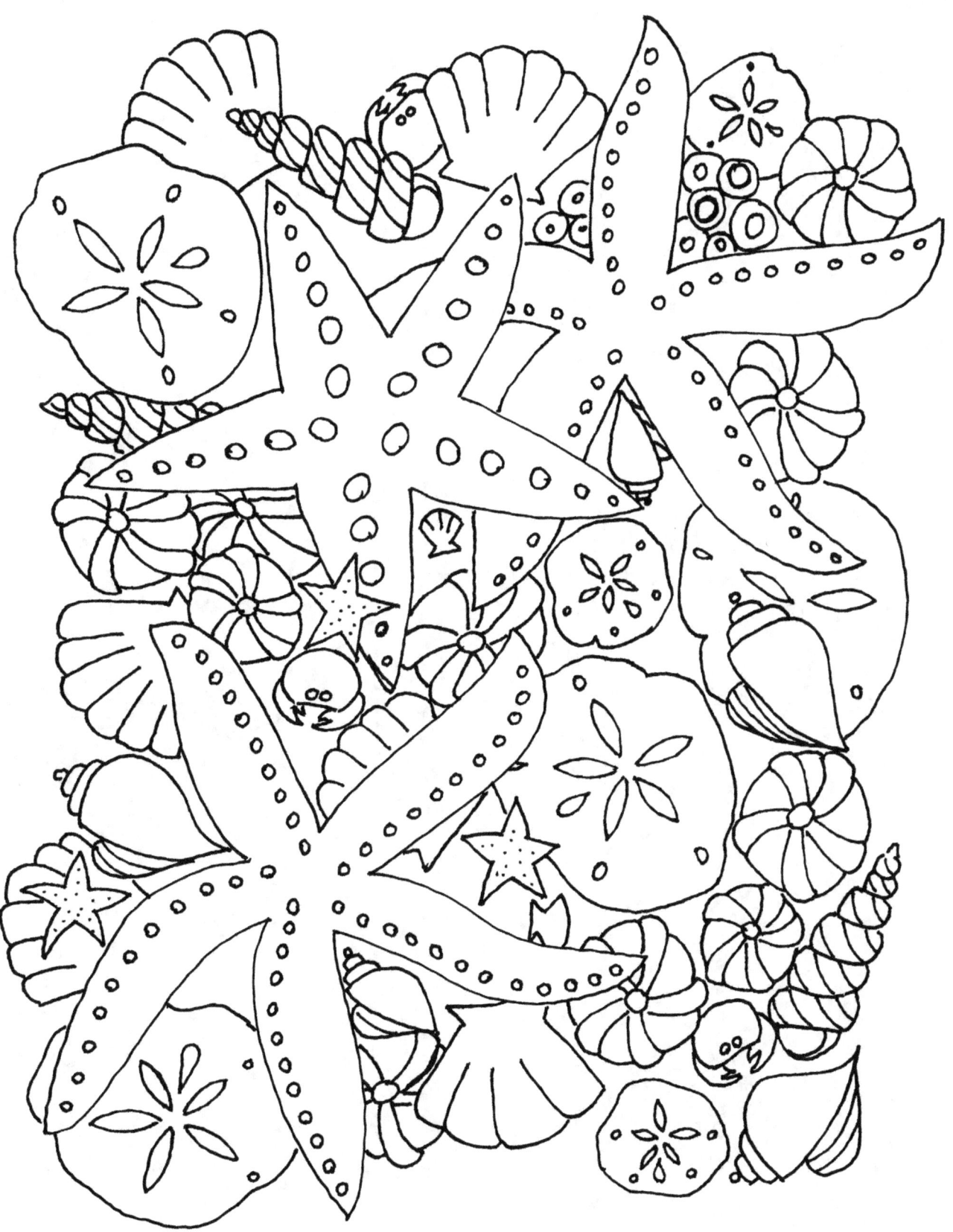

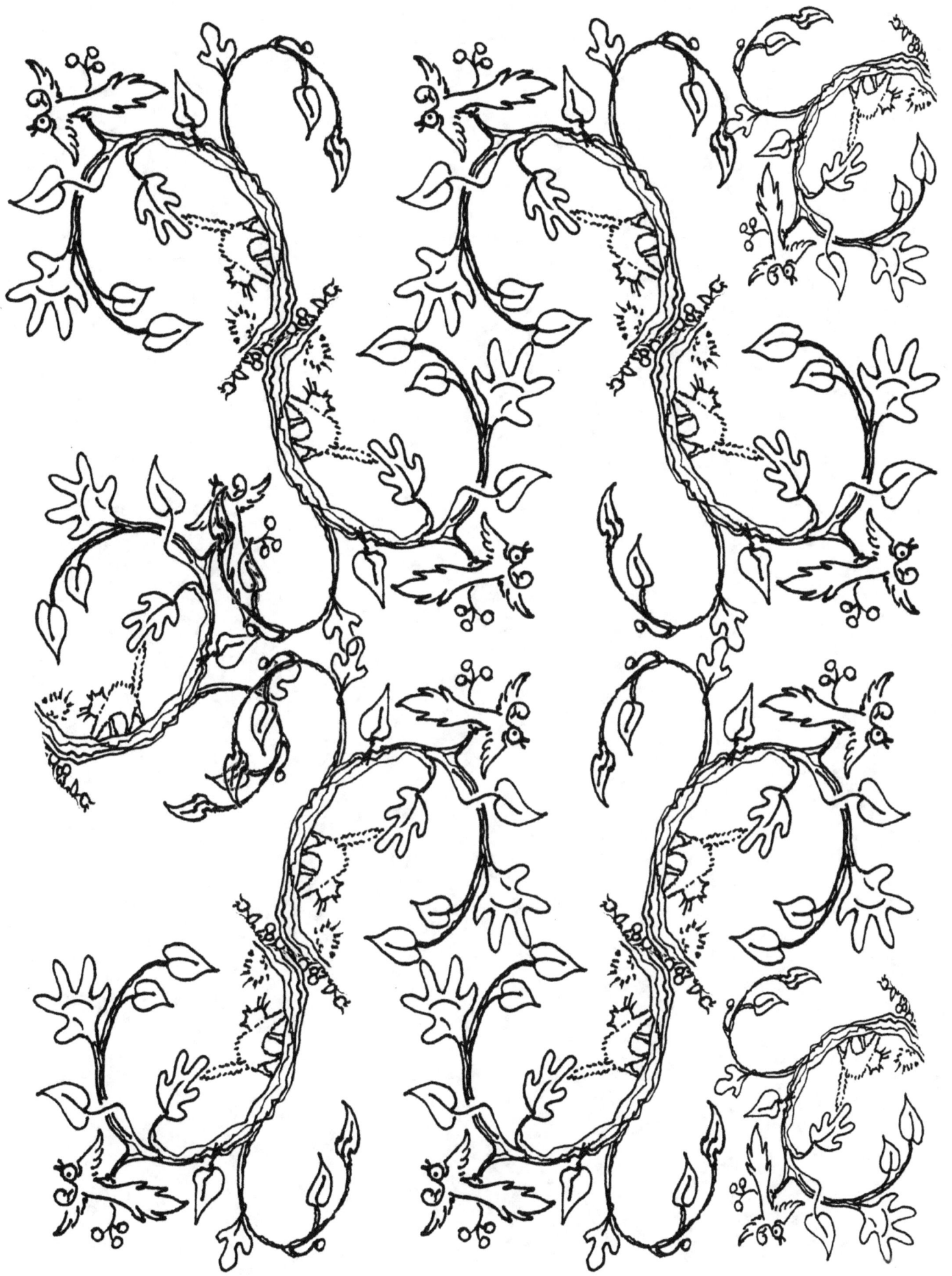

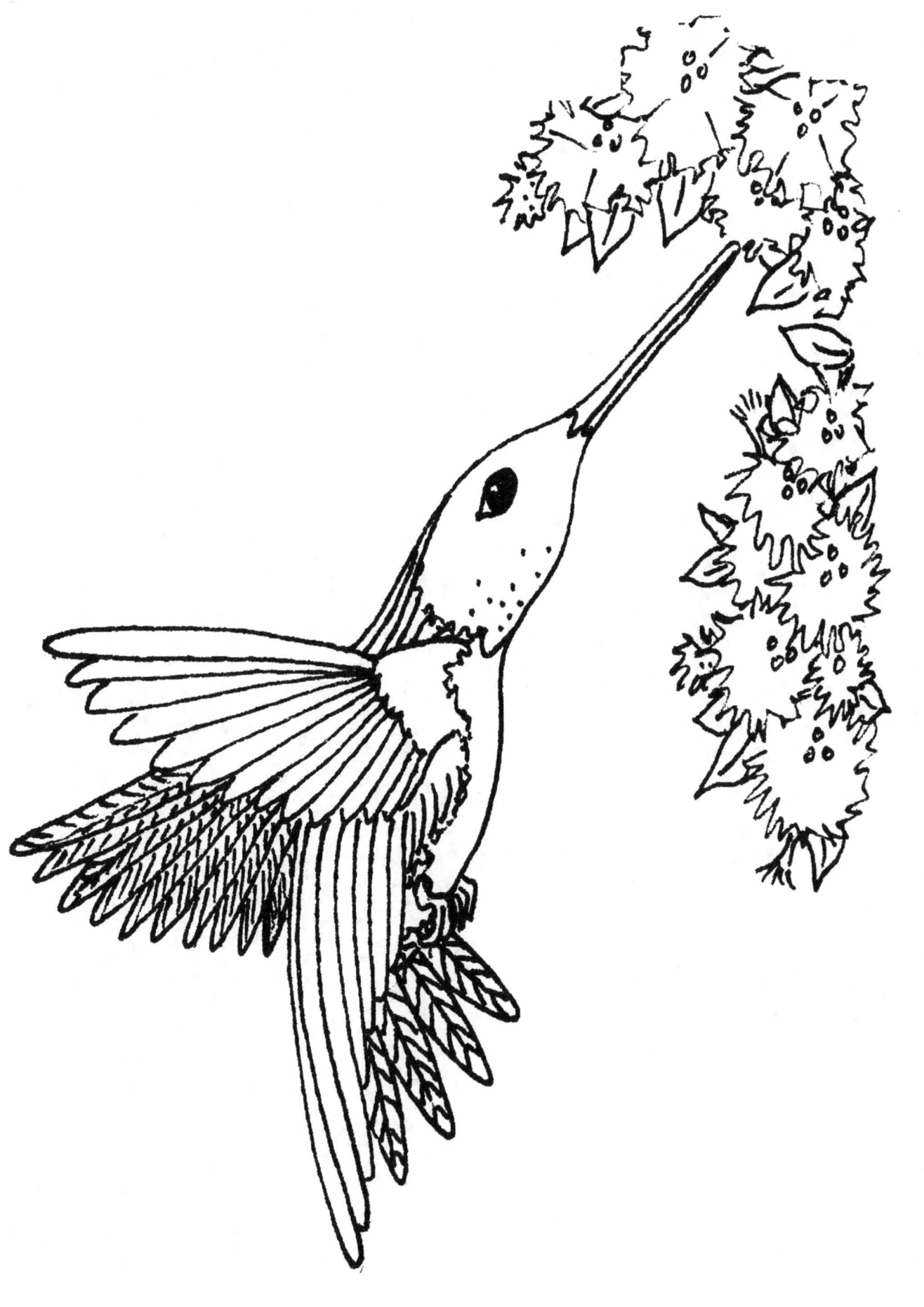

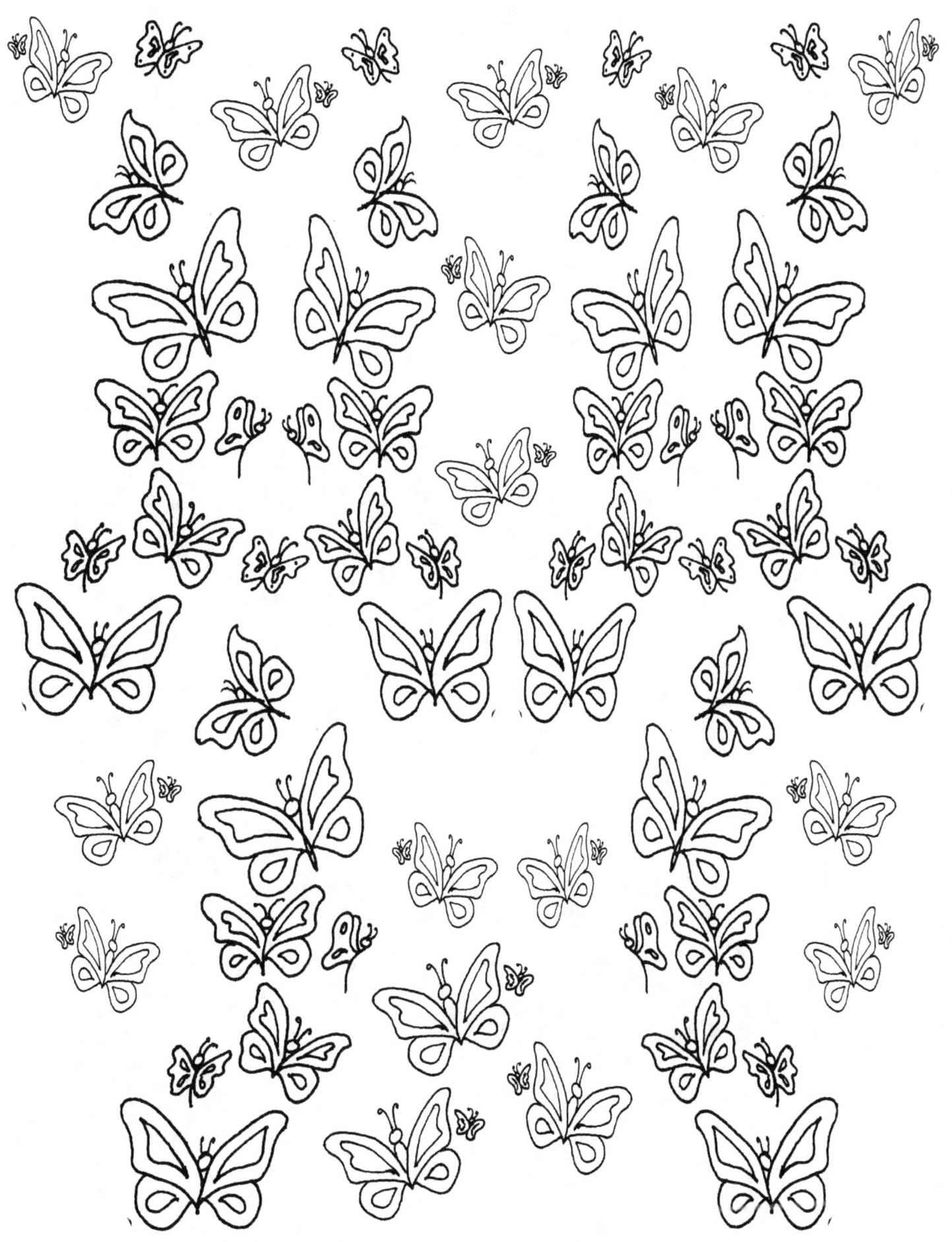

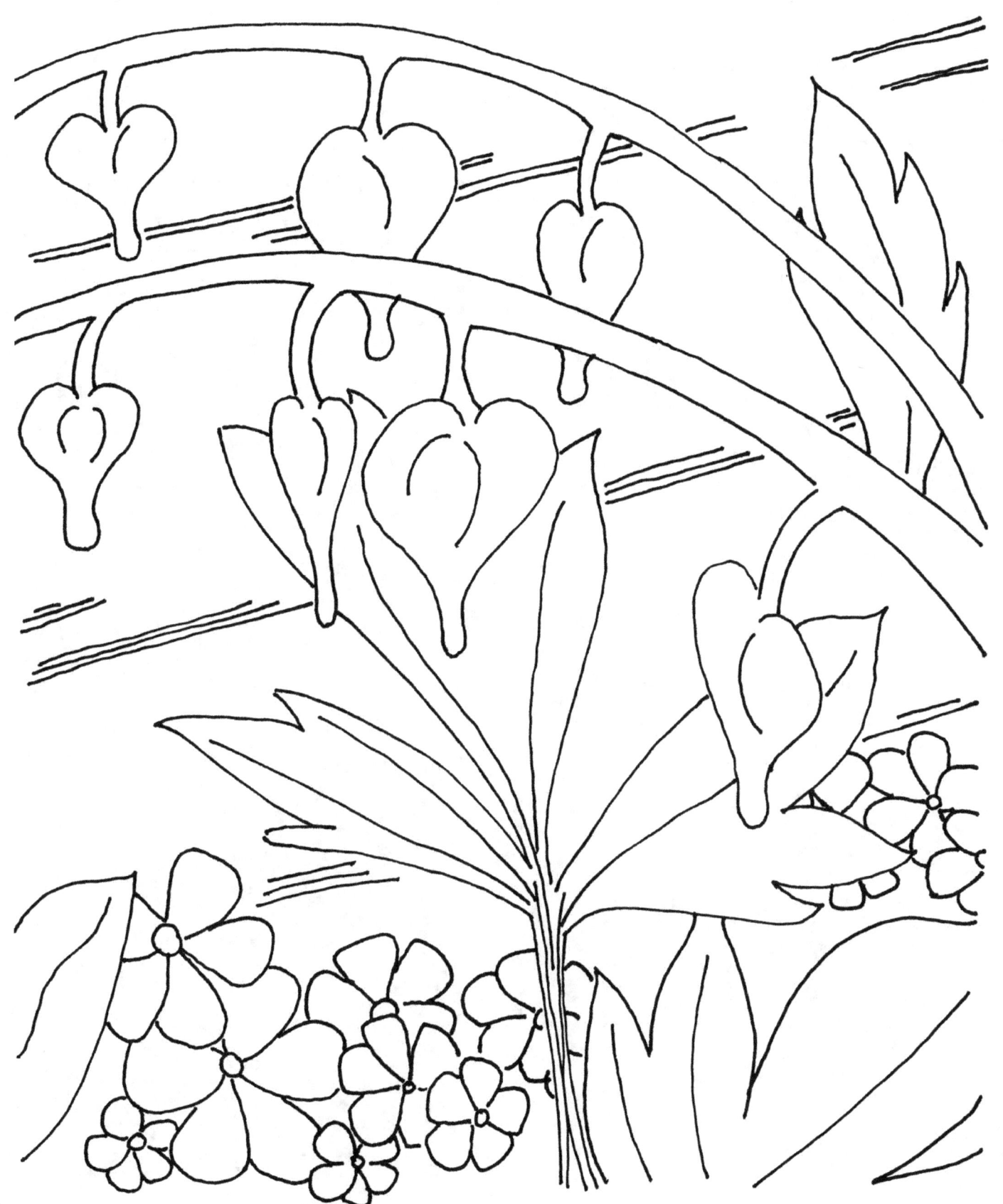

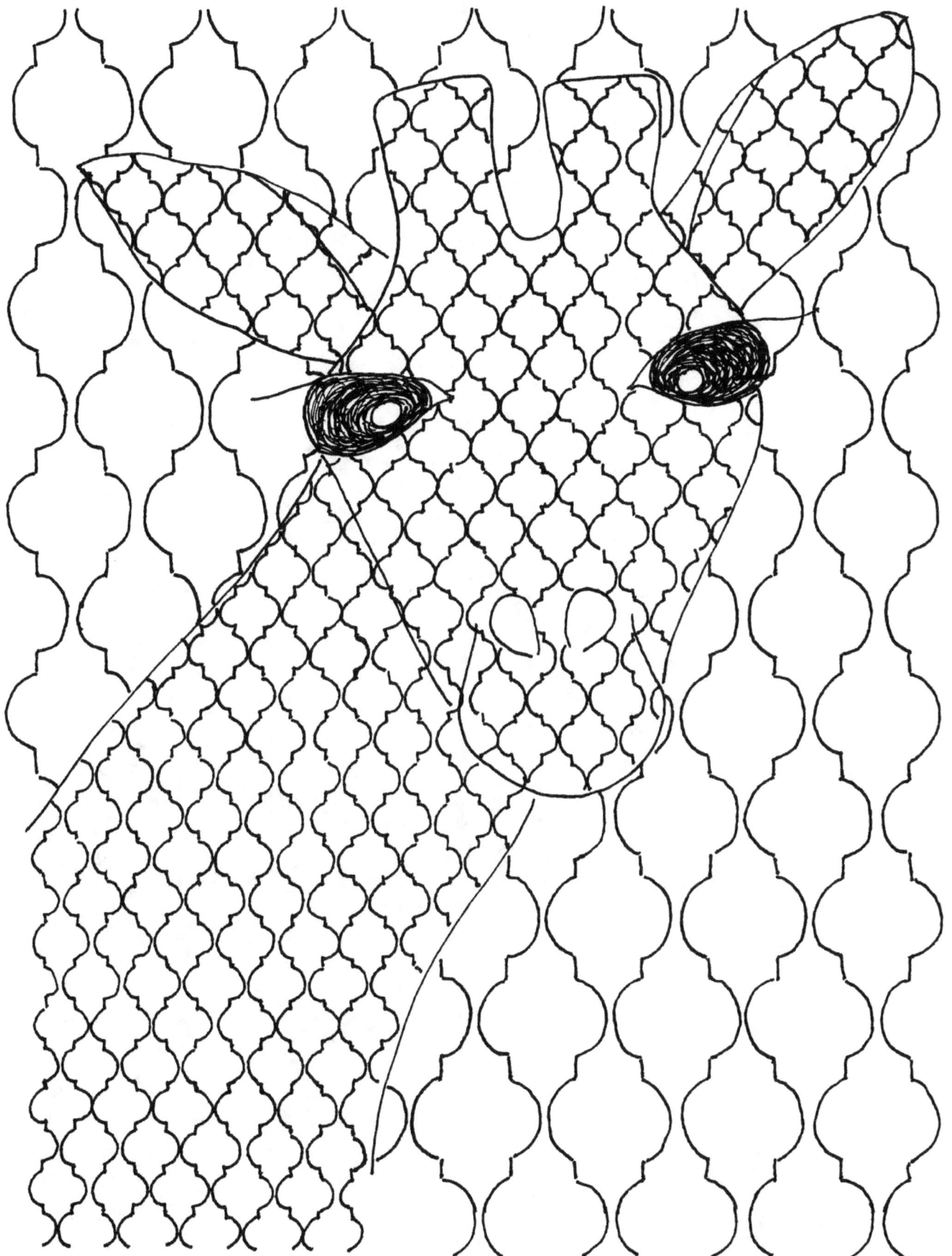

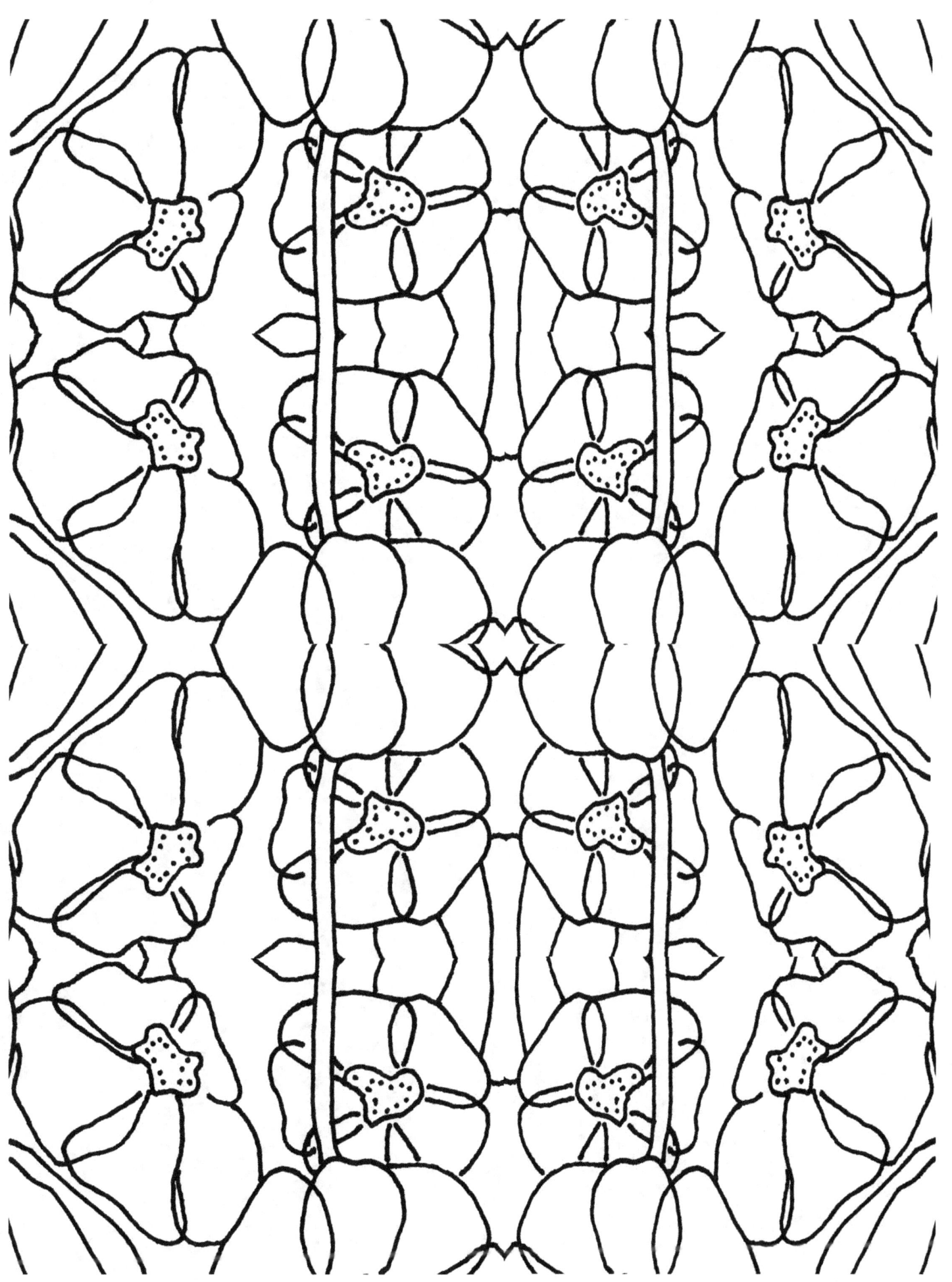

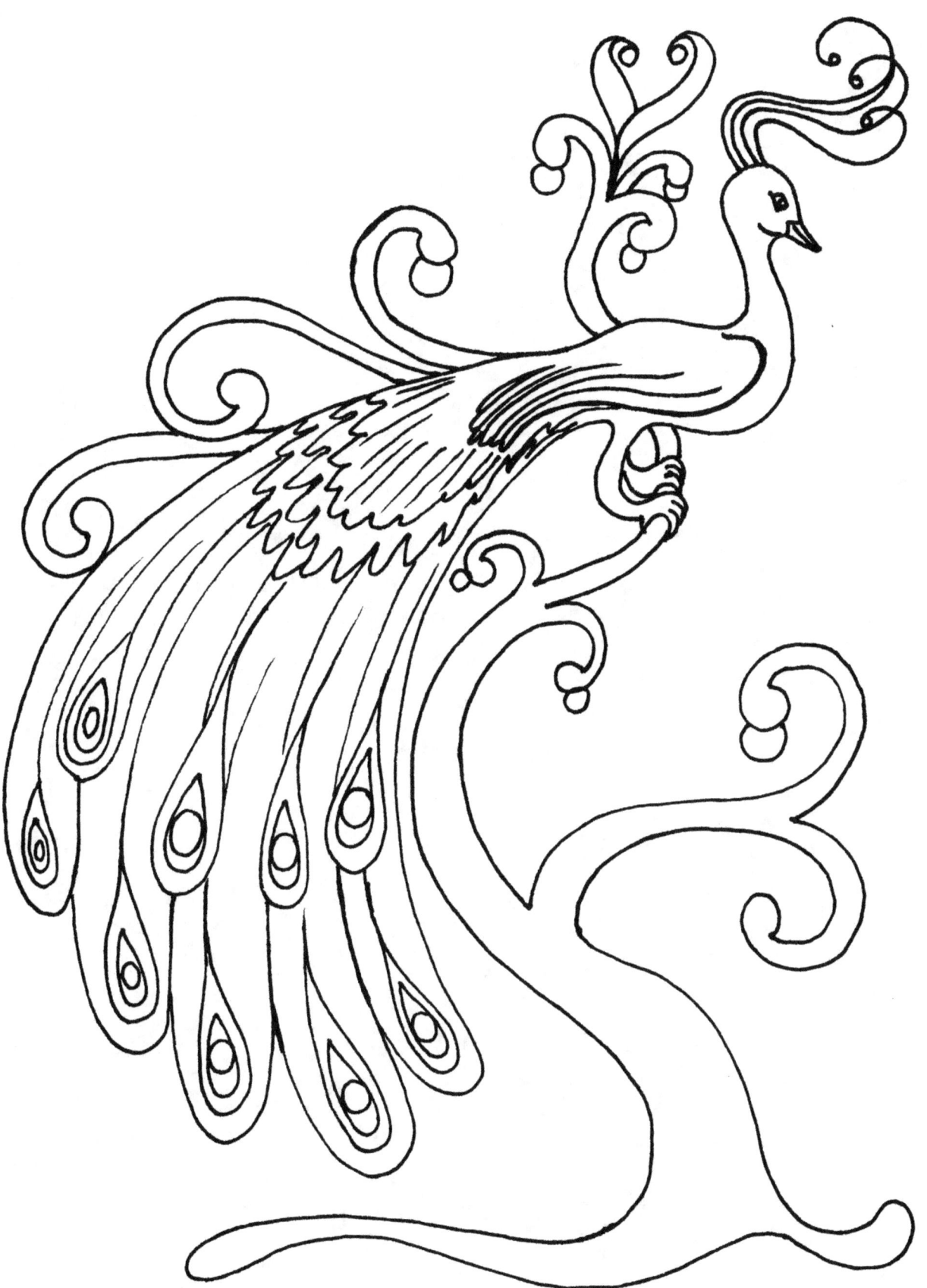

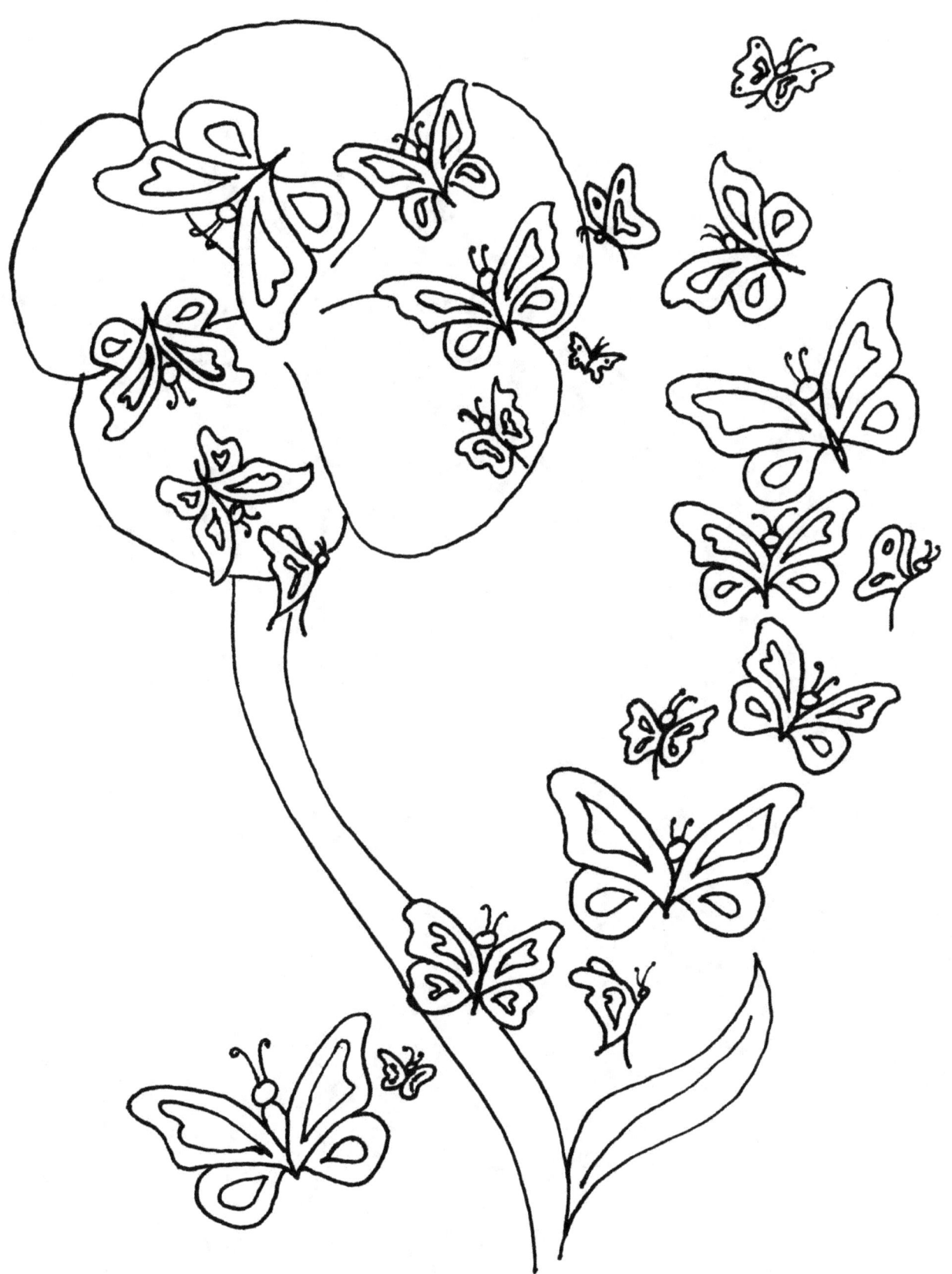

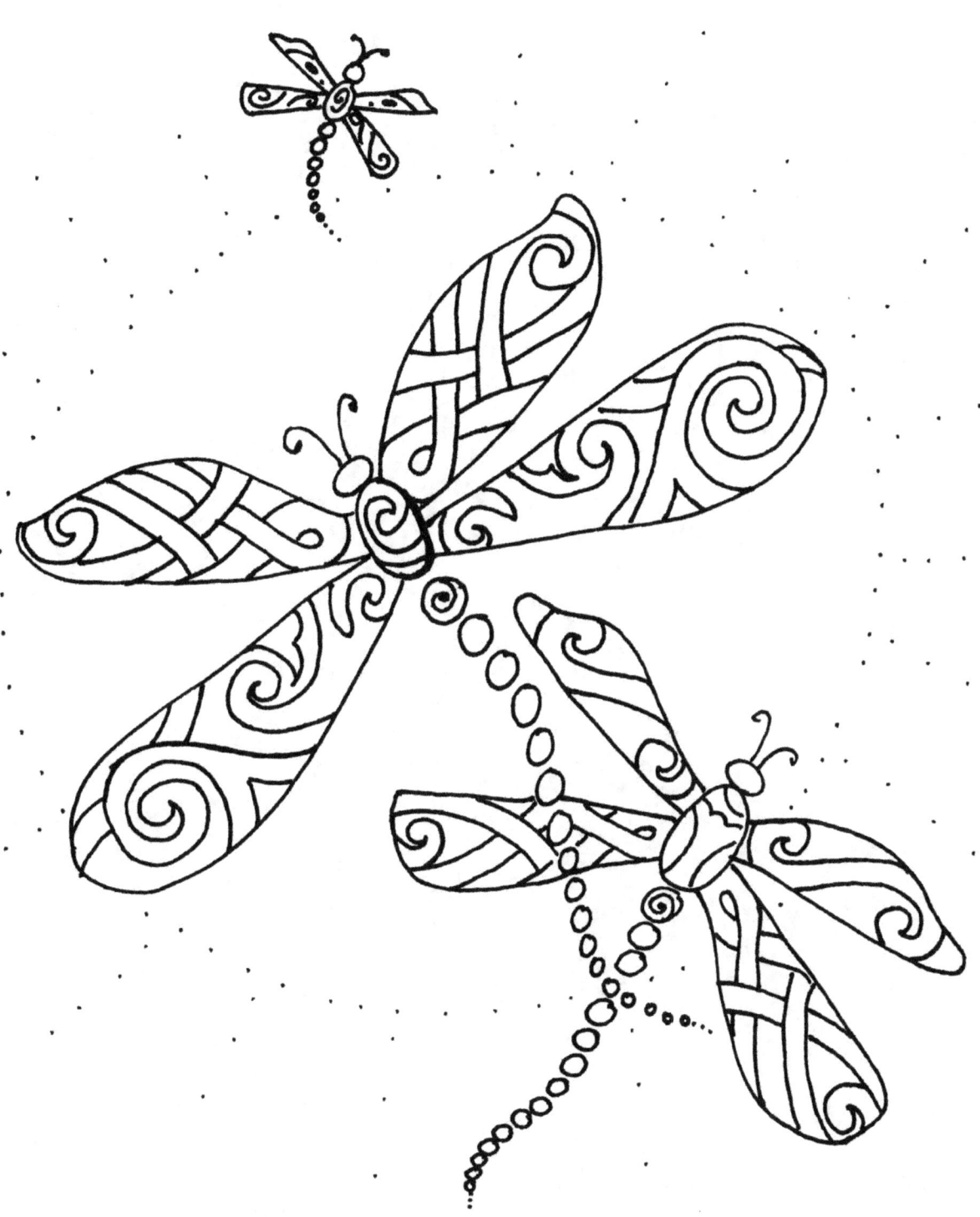

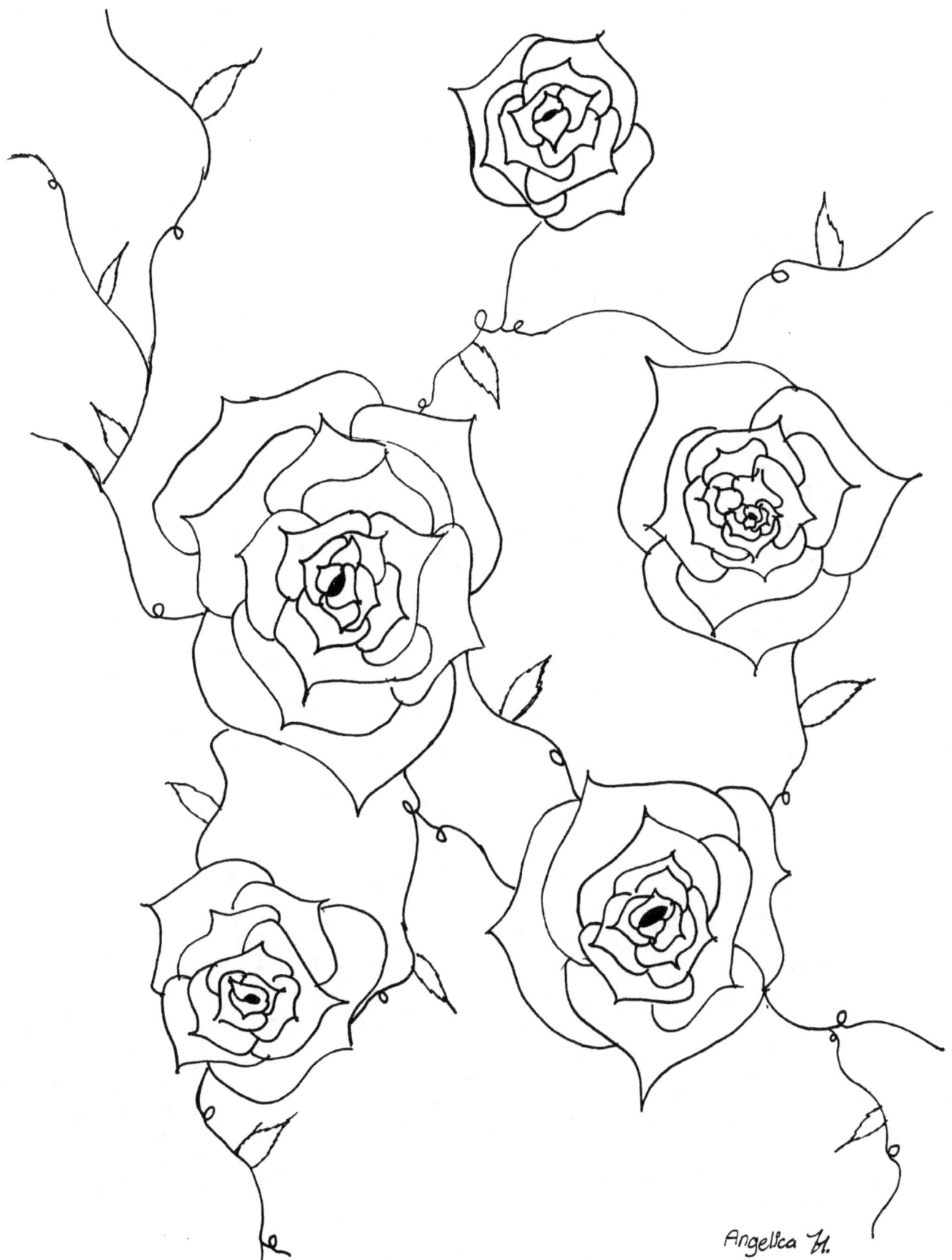

Angelica M.

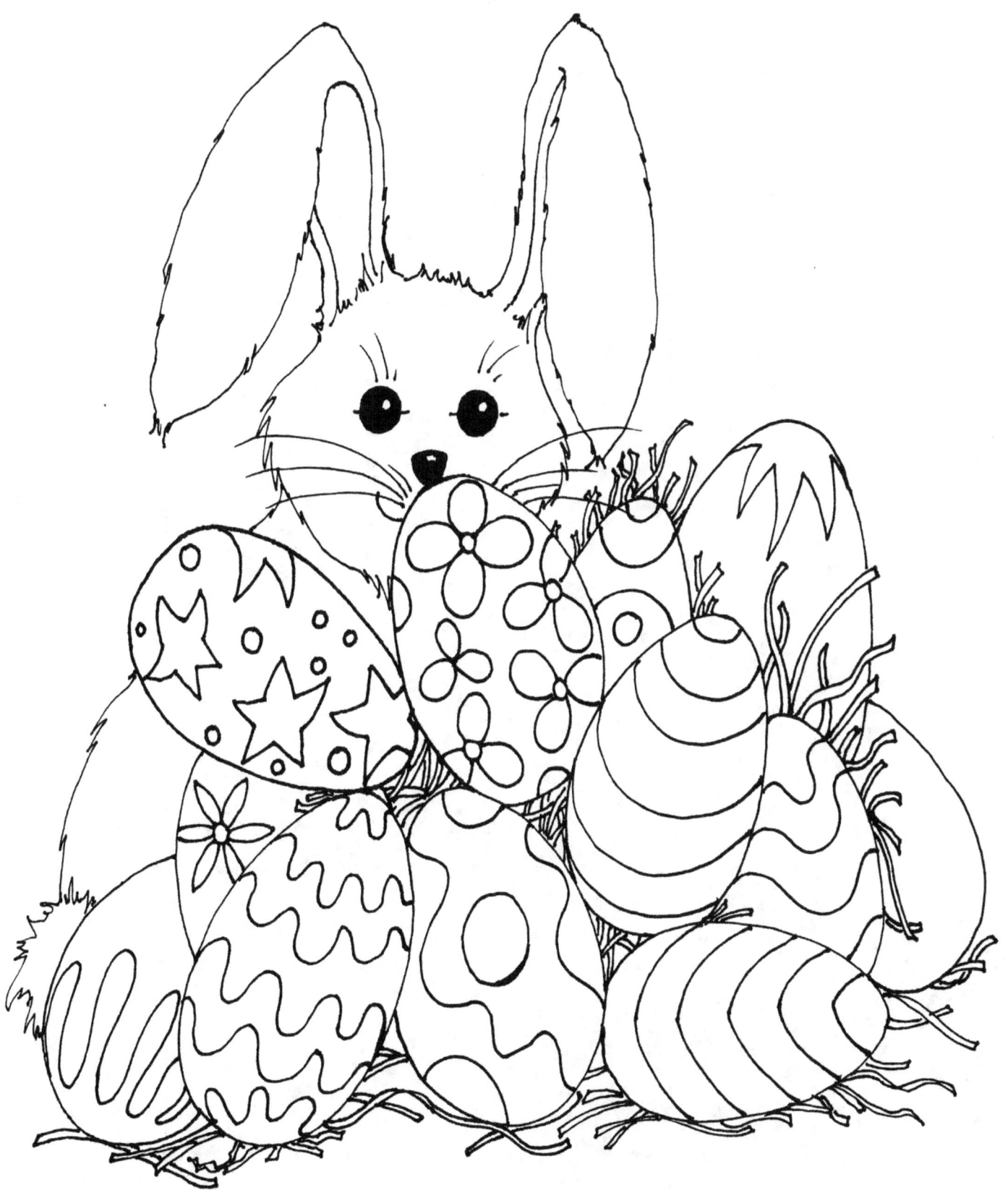

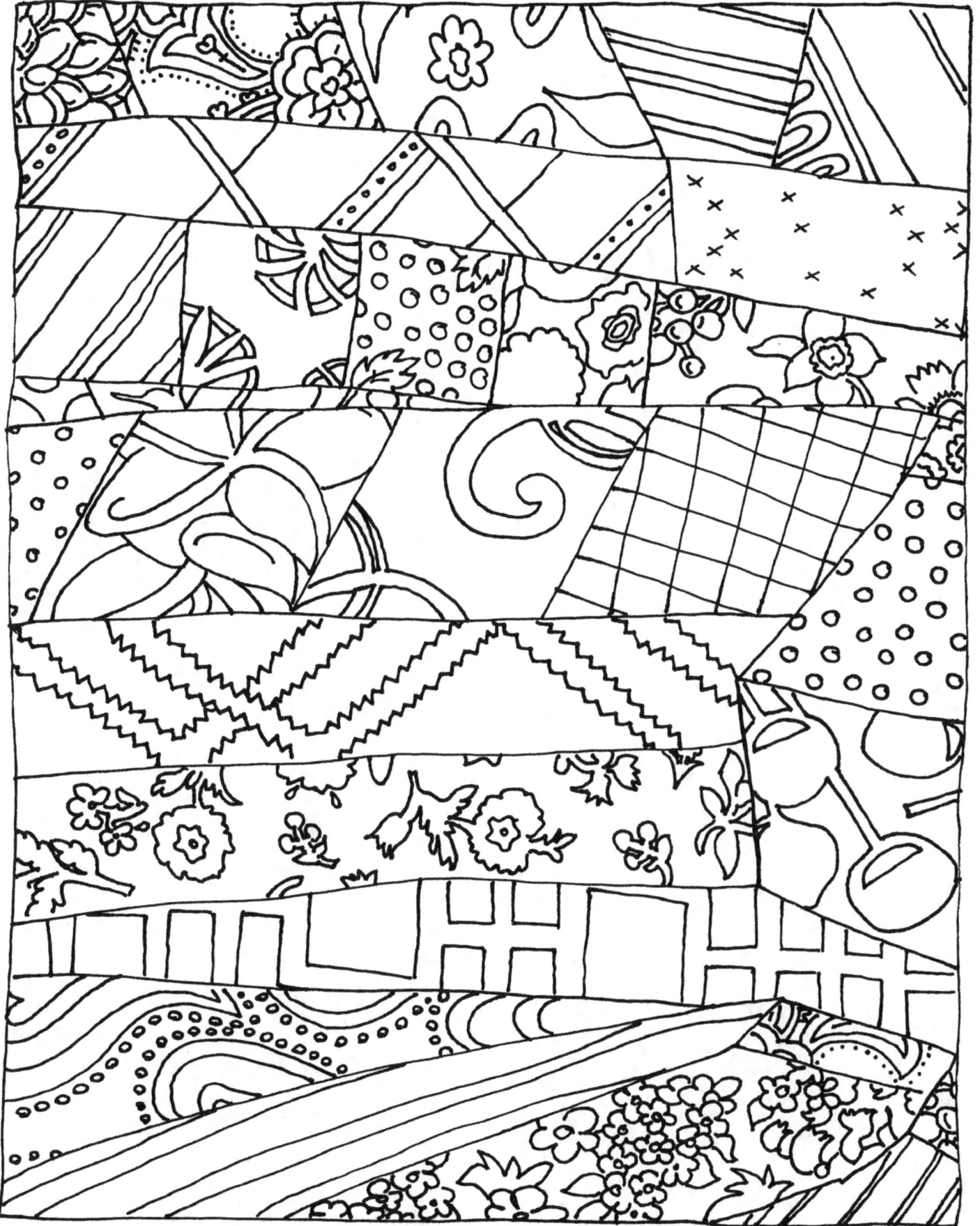

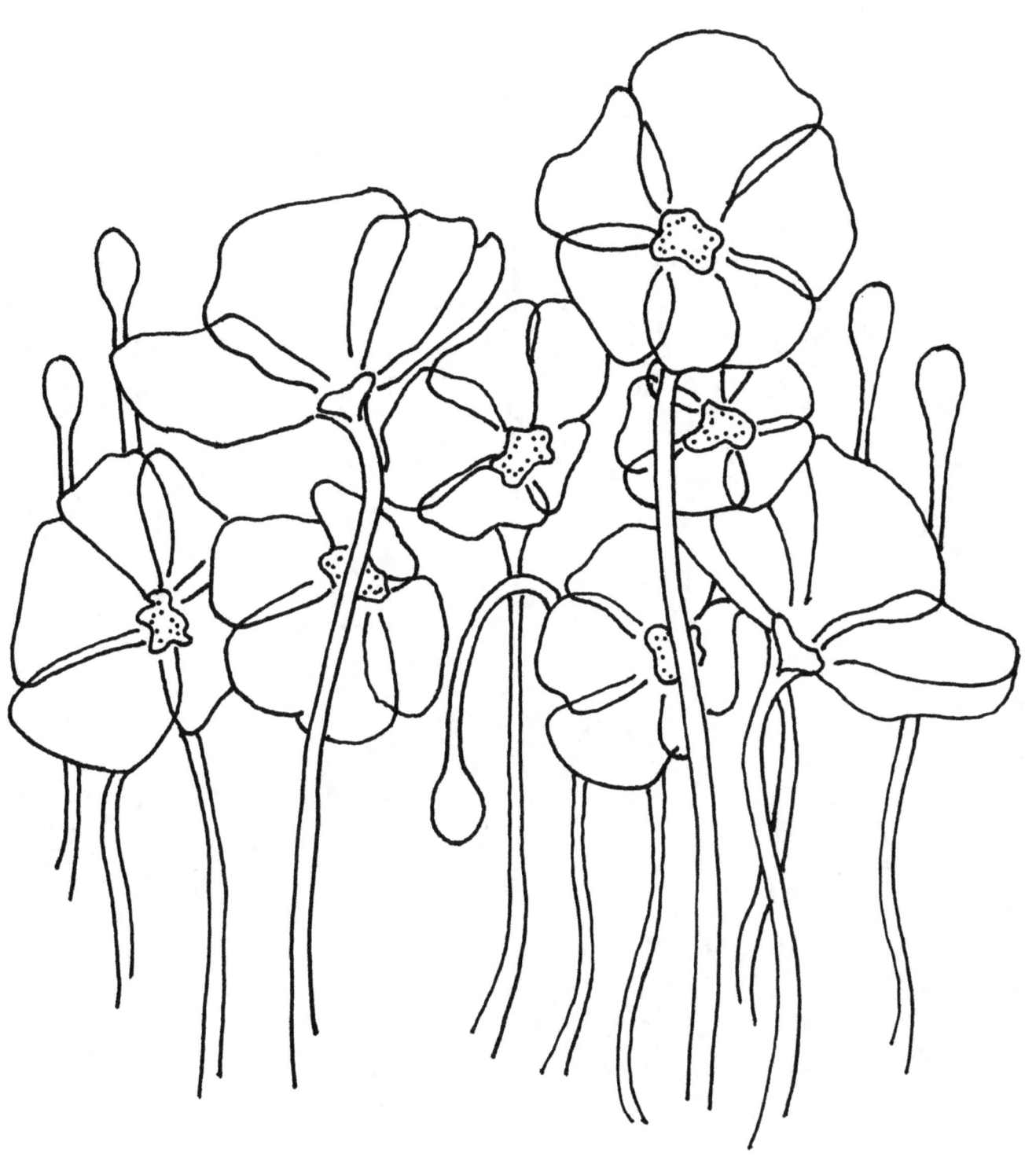

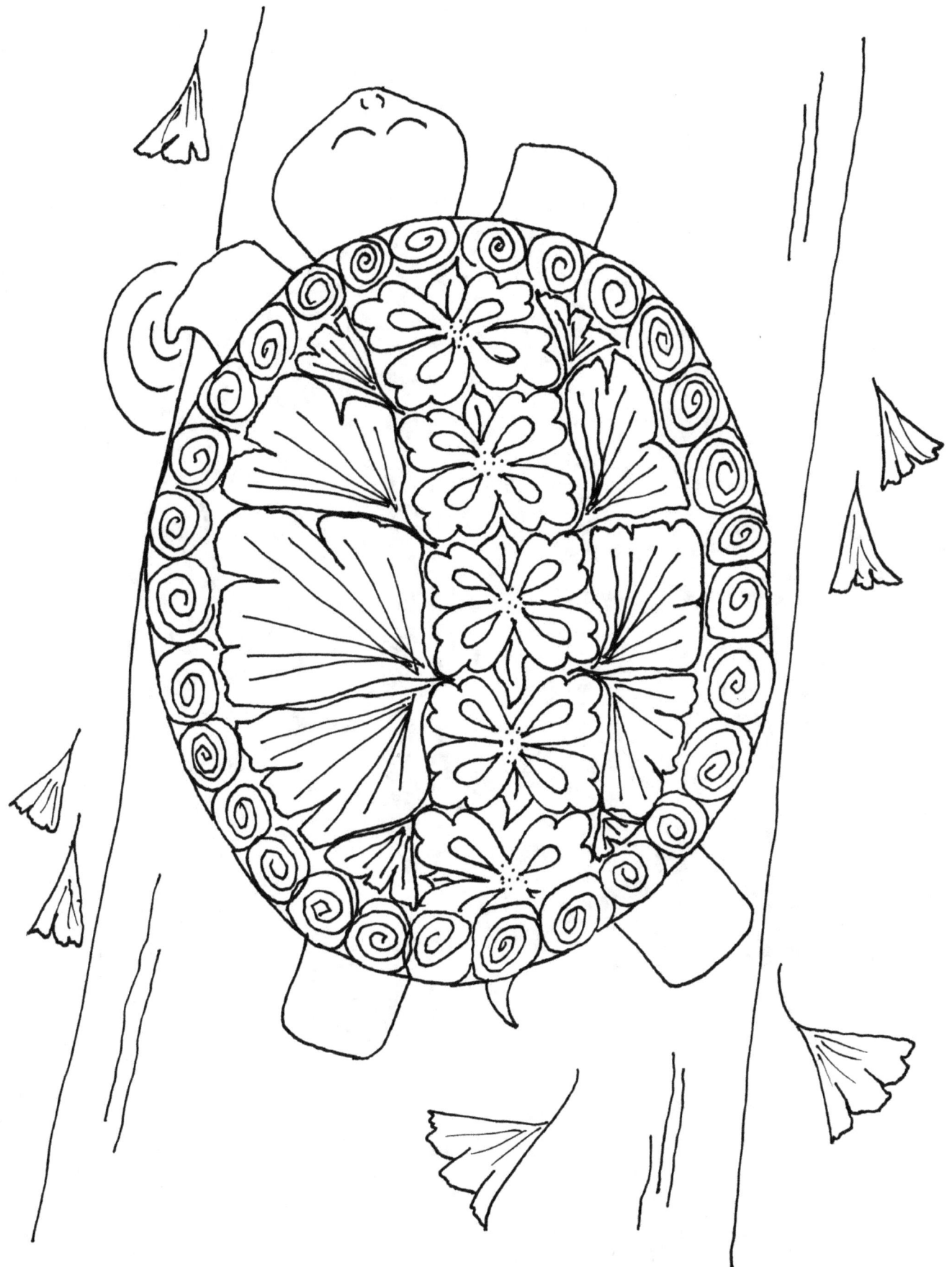

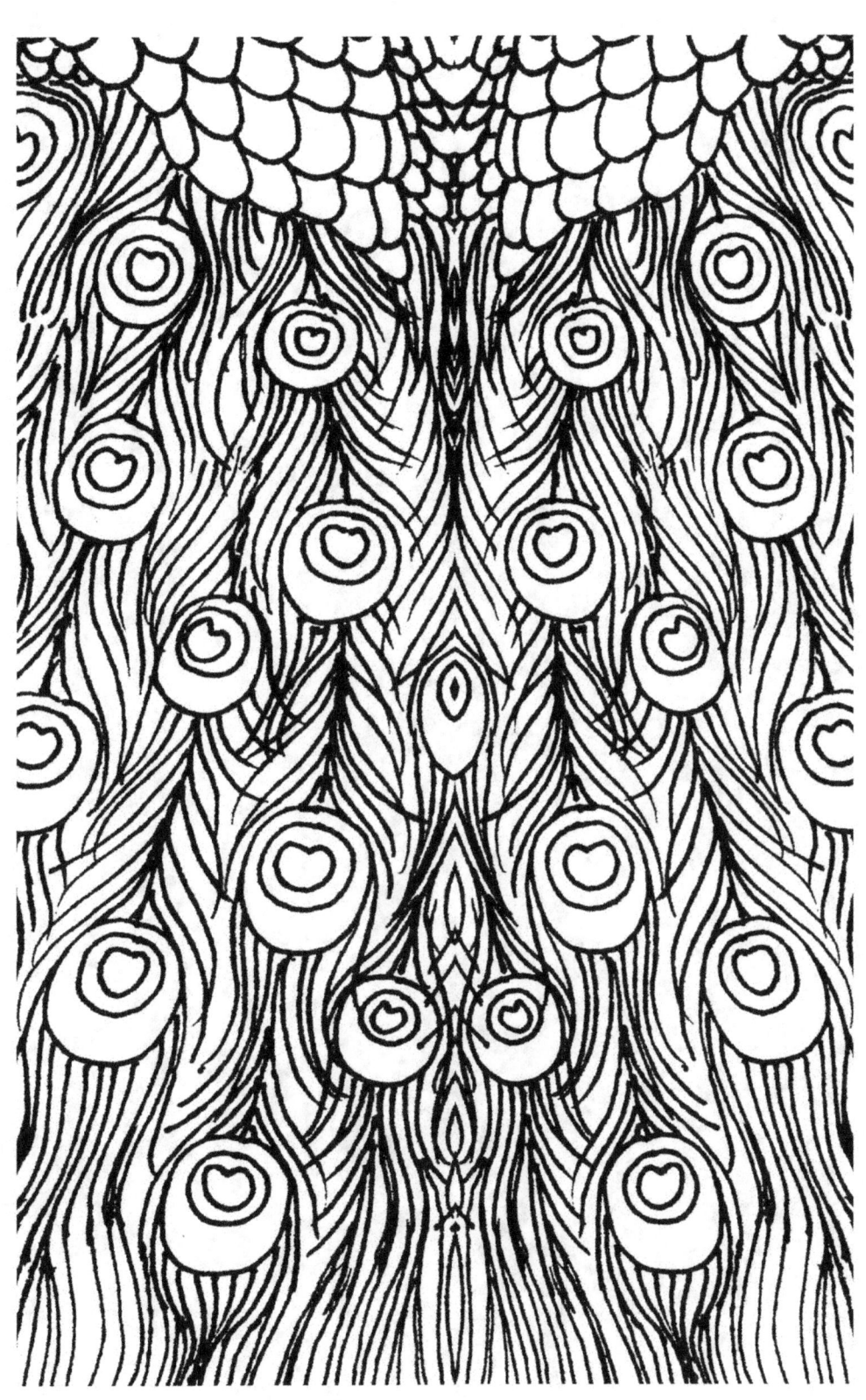

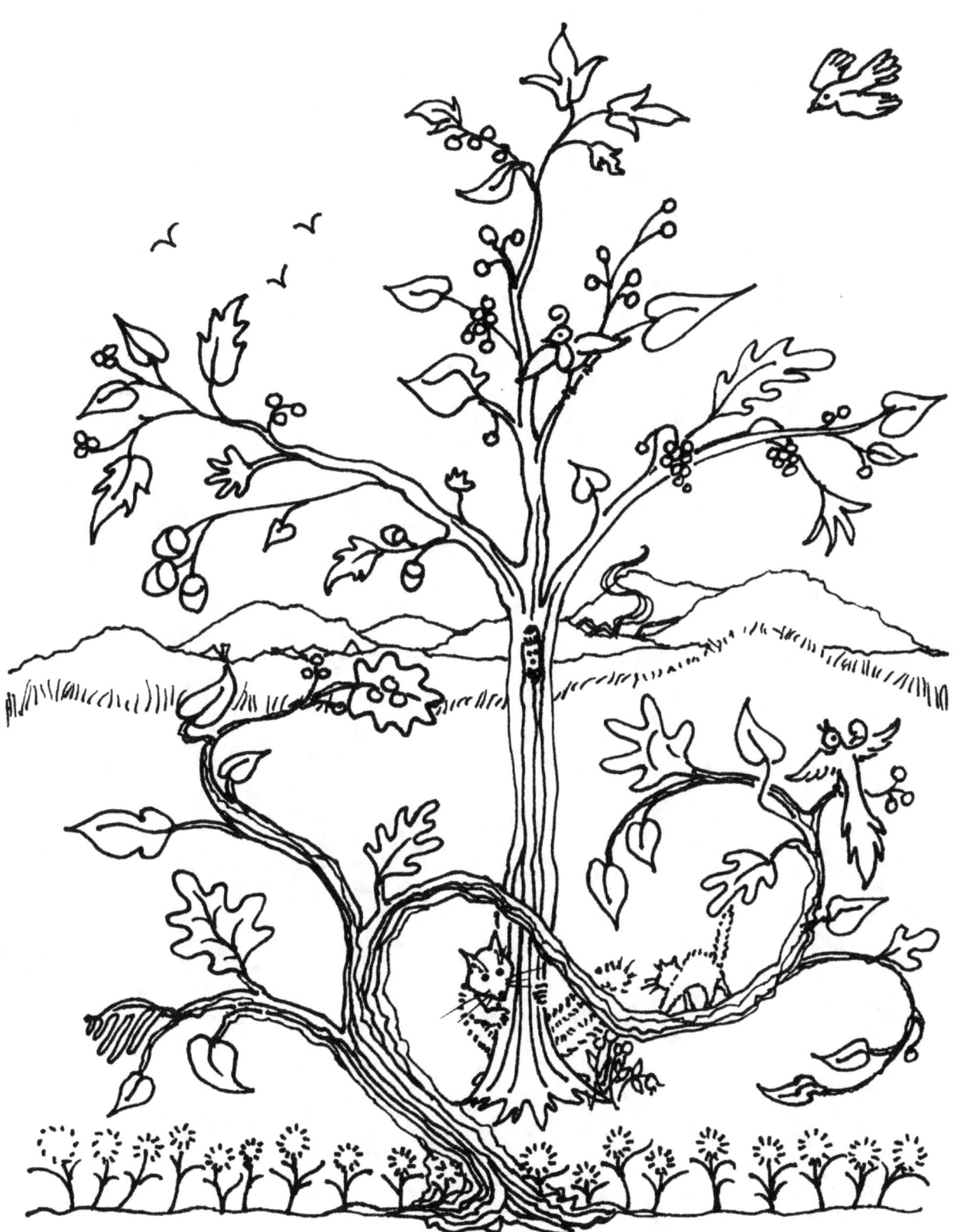

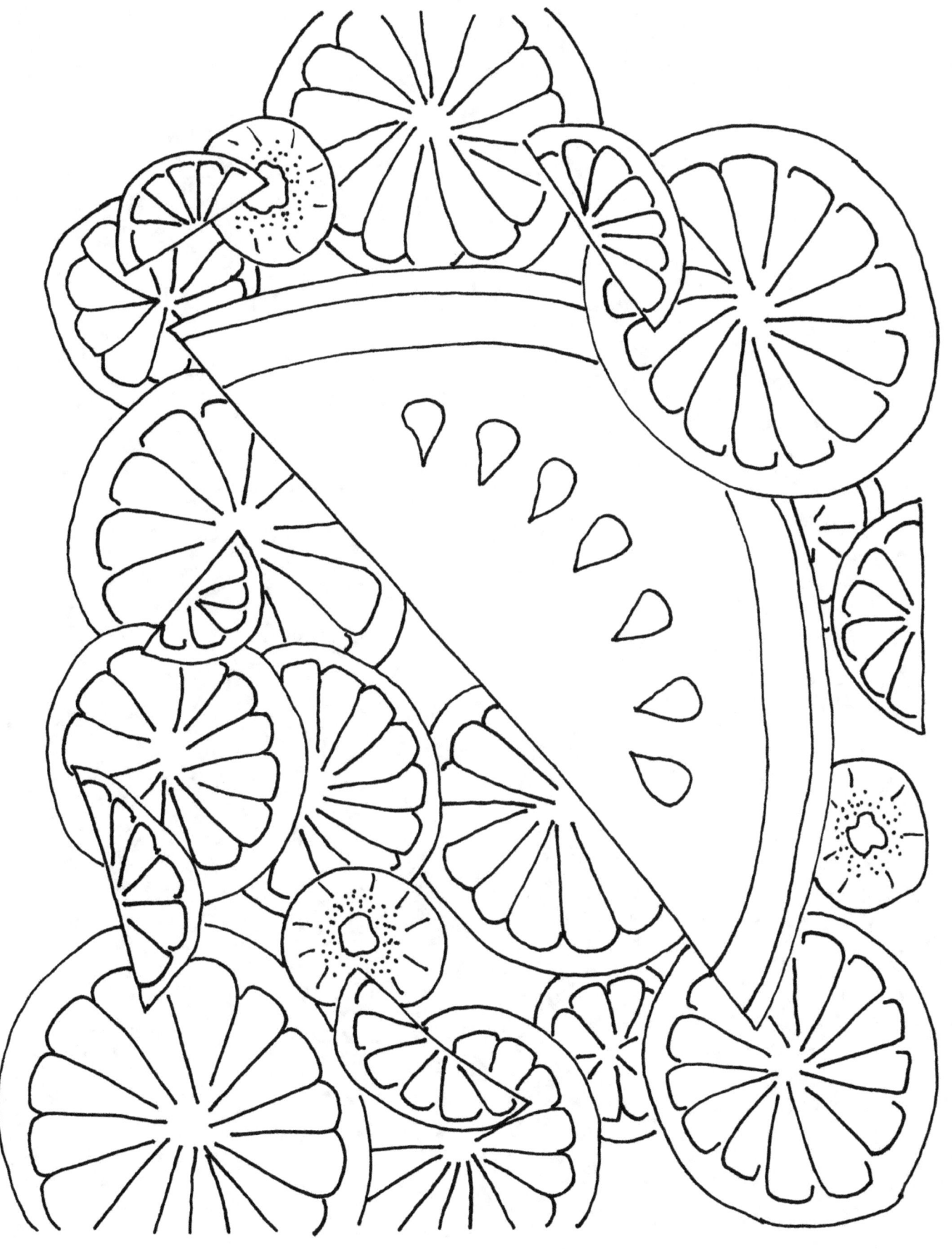

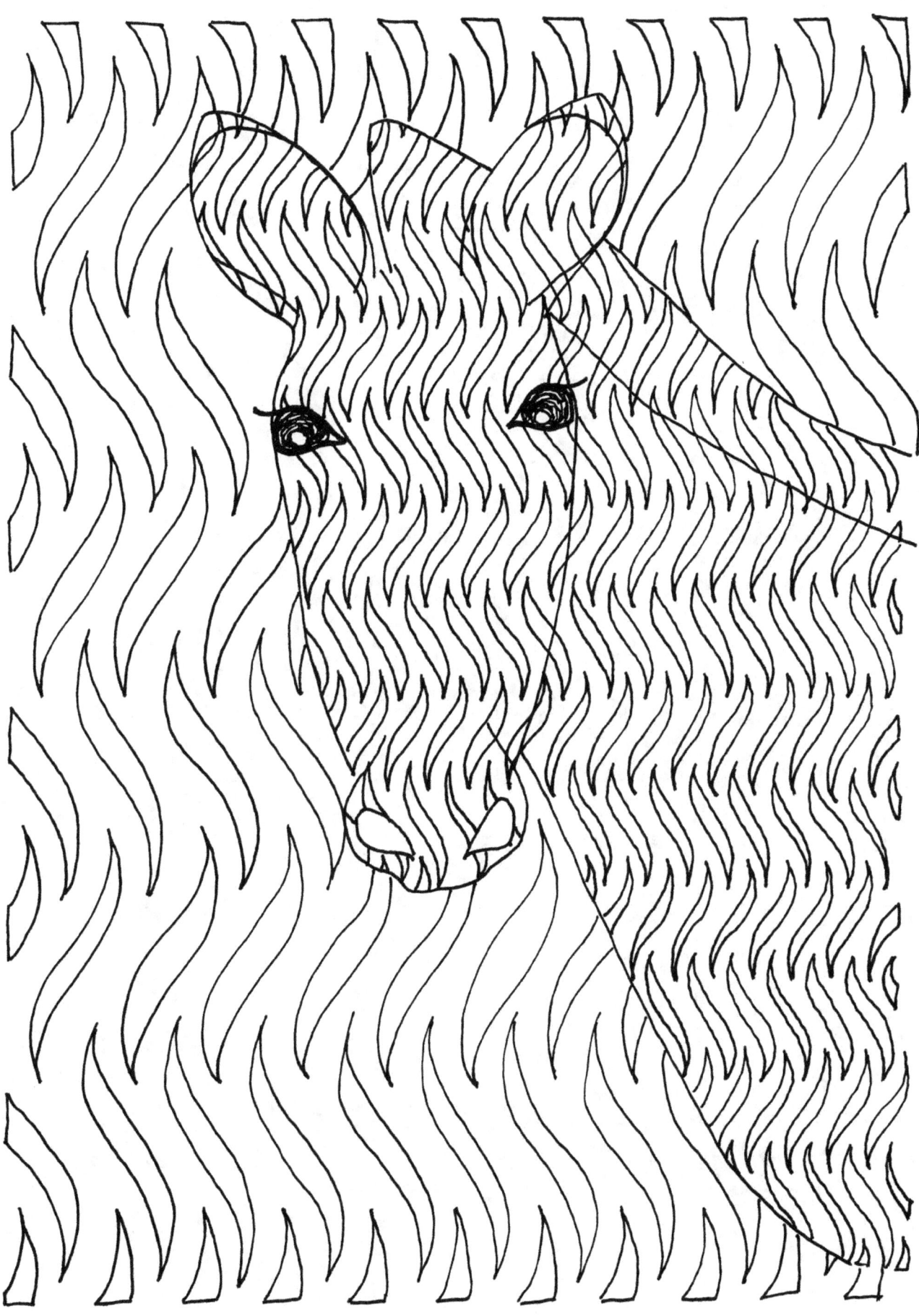

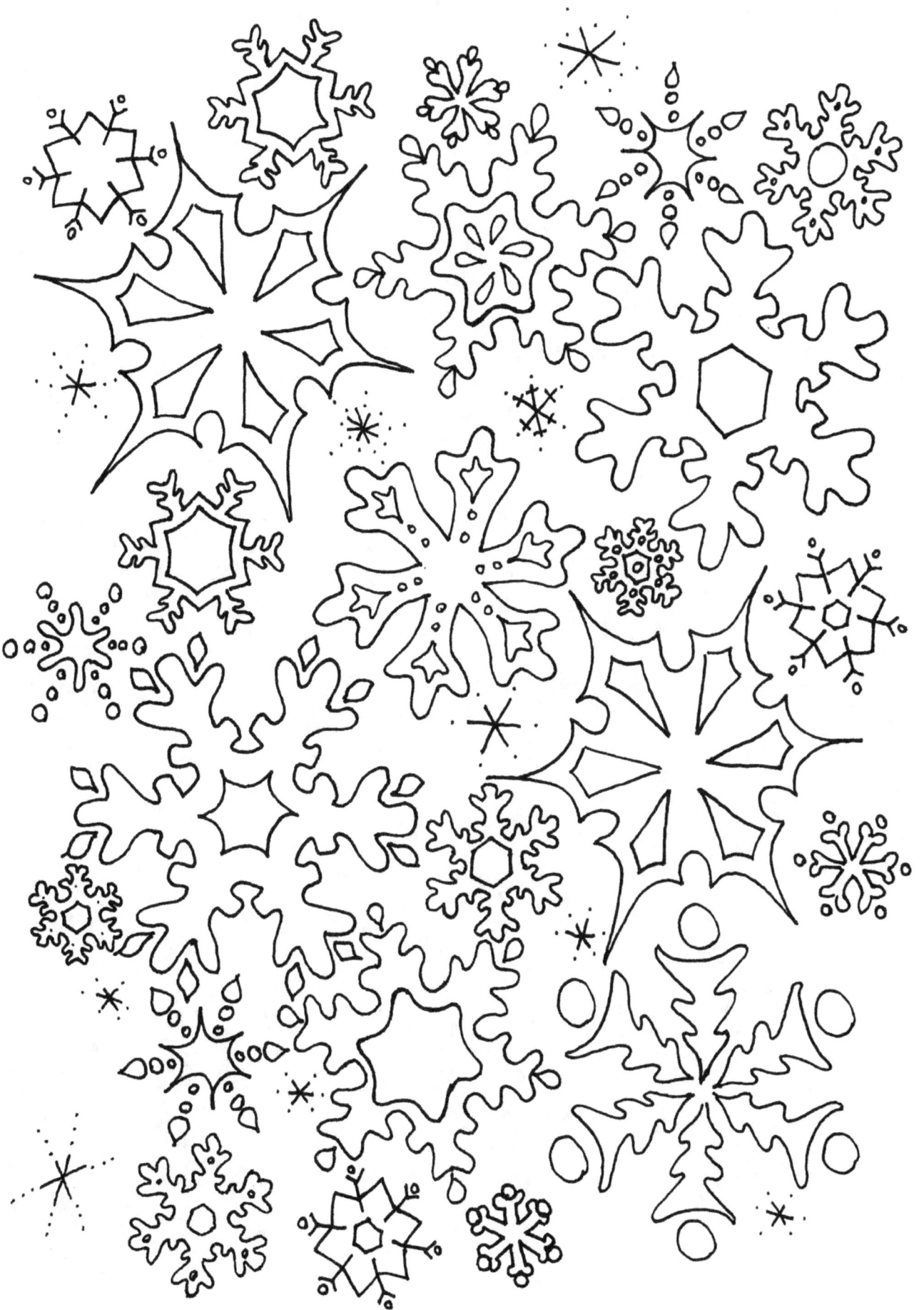

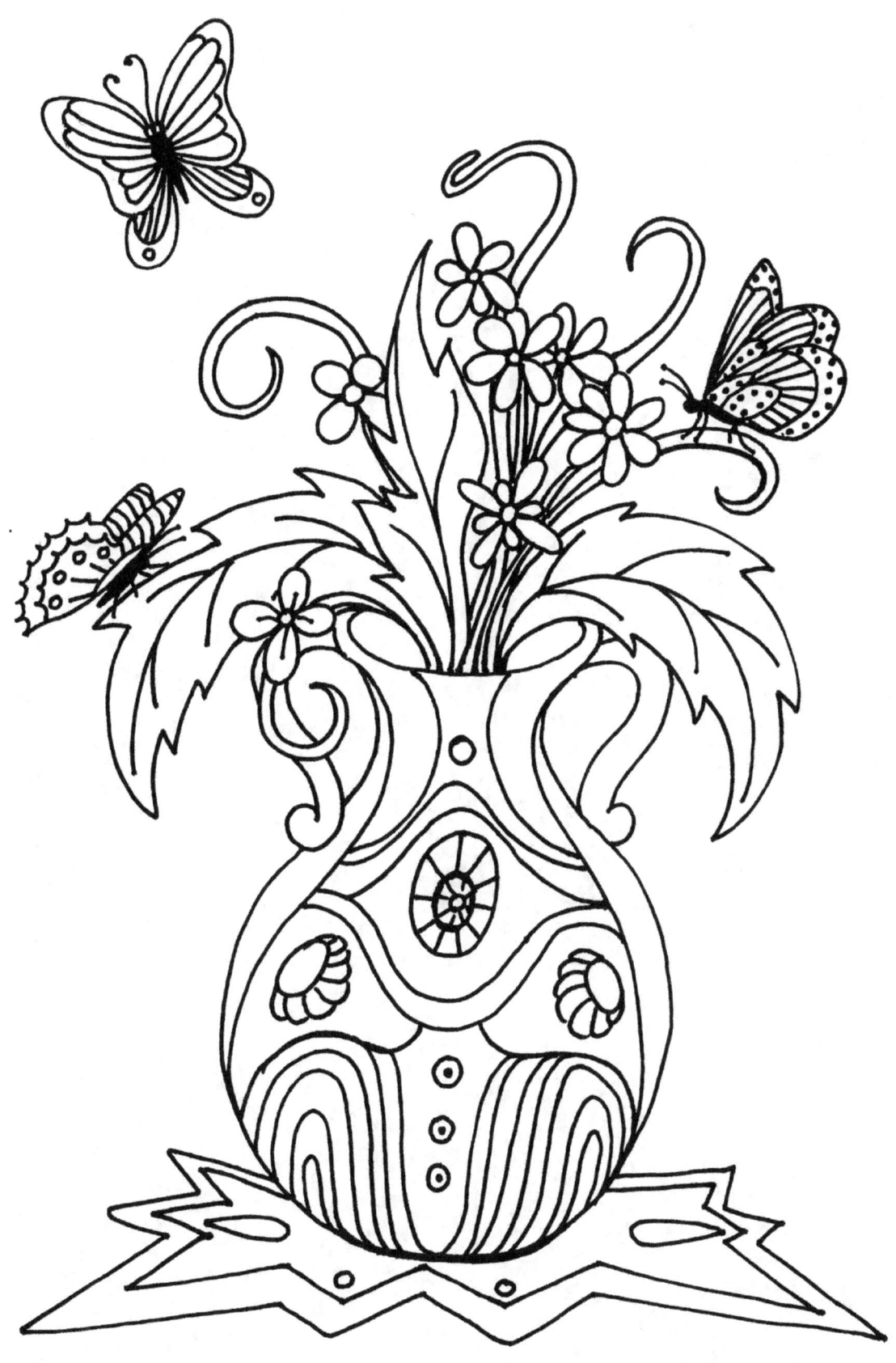

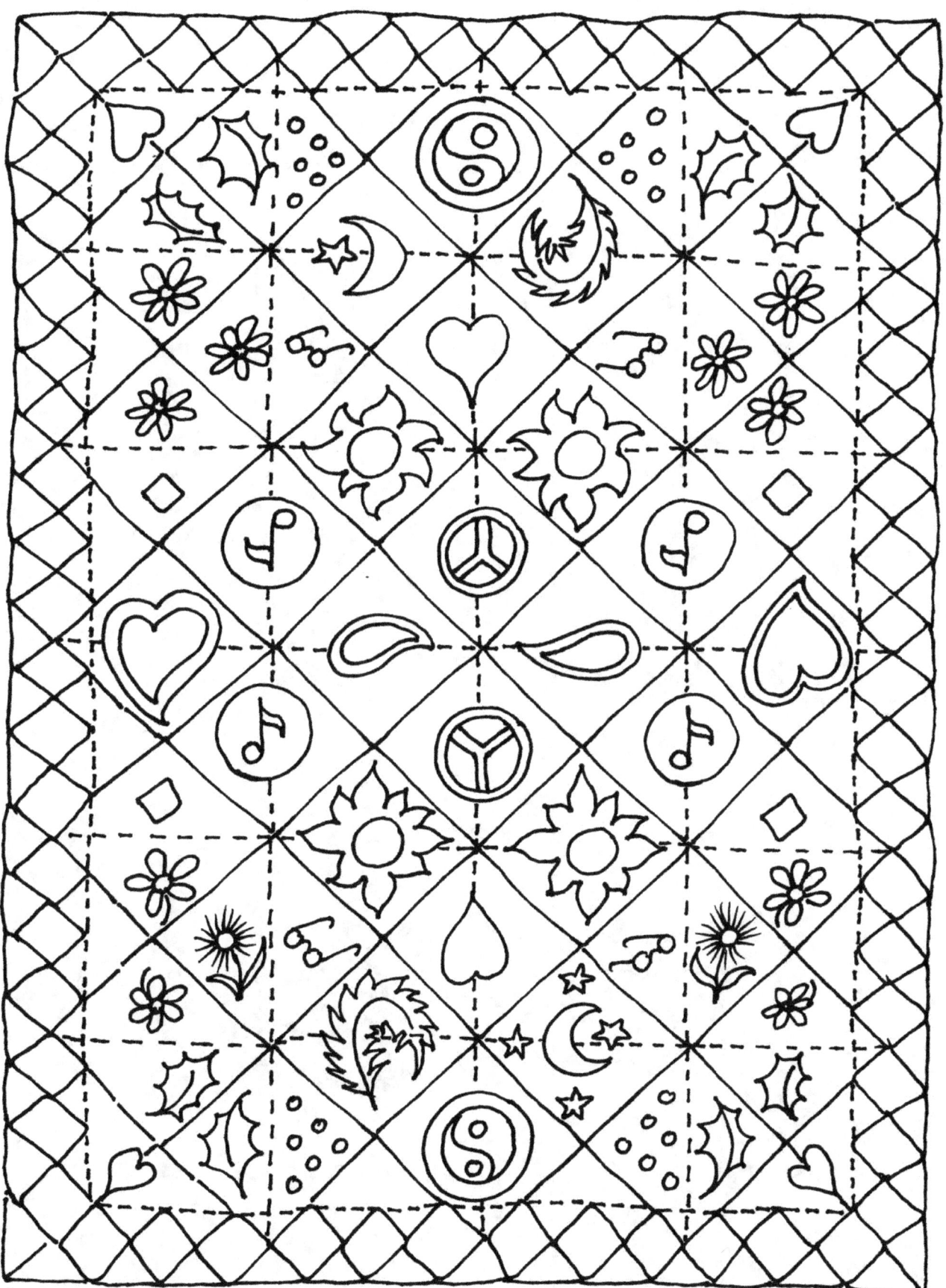

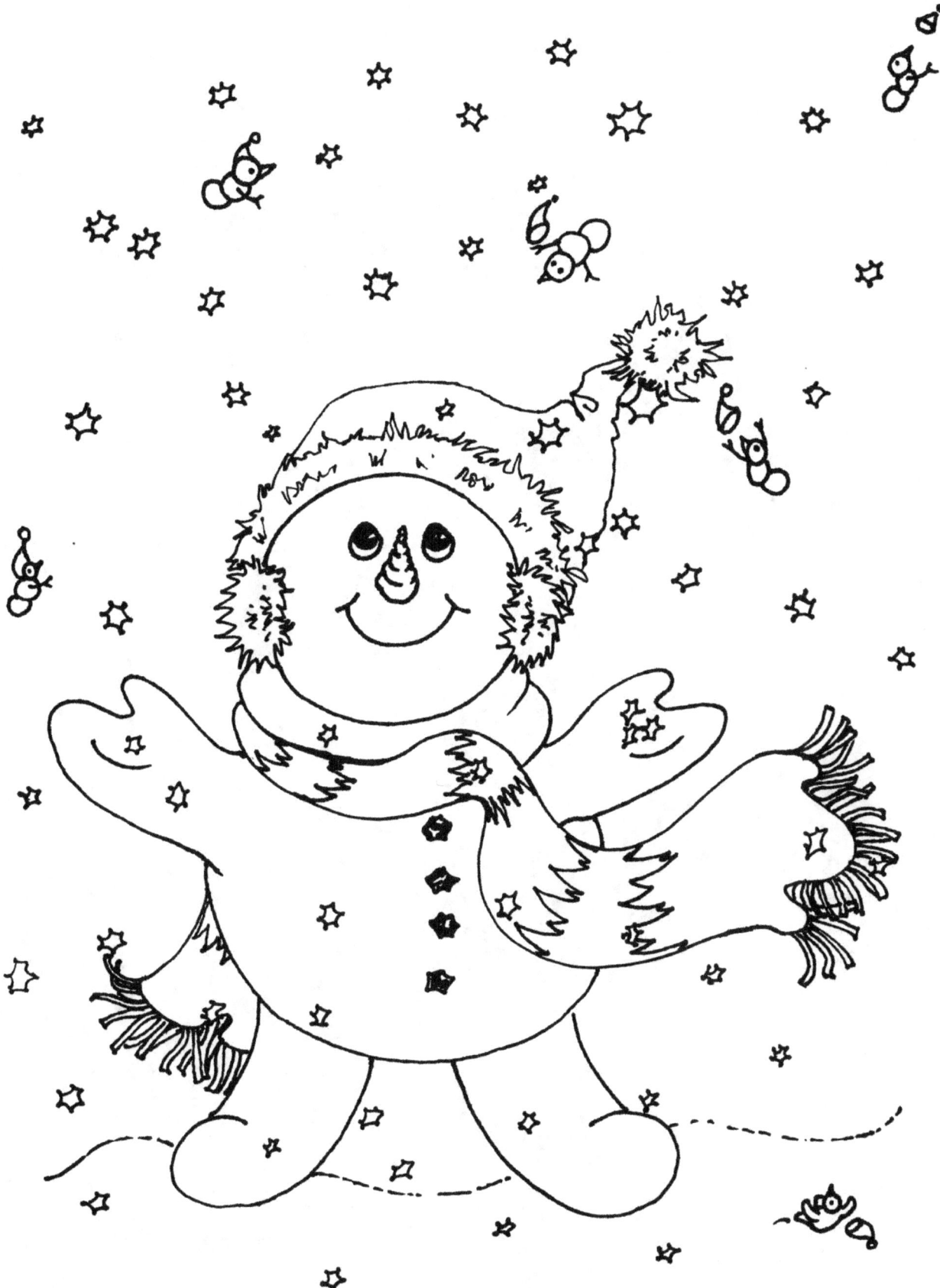

Meet the Illustrators

Louise Bremer is the illustrator of the children's book "Oodles and Skoodles of Friends" by Jan Luck and Linda Barboa. She is also a Juried Artist and Member of the Best of Missouri Hands. Her father had a degree in art education, and his encouragement and artistic suggestions led her to study art in college and beyond. She draws, paints, creates costumes, and has passed her skills and love of creating on to her children and grandchildren.

Kristina Heth has a Master's Degree in Speech Language Pathology (MS. CCC-SLP). She has over 20 years experience helping people regain abilities lost due to Parkinson's disease, Alzheimer's disease, Dementia, and Stroke. Her illustrations can be found at her Etsy store (https:www.etsy.com/shop/Coloring Cocktails) and her illustrated therapy materials can be found in her Teachers Pays Teachers store (https://teacherspaysteachers/Store/Kristina-Heth).Thanks to the encouragement and skills passed down from her mother, Louise Bremer, she also paints, sculpts, and creates with metals and hot glass.

Angelica Heth has a colorful and creative personality and expresses herself by painting on walls, drawing Manga, creating fashion, writing music and singing. Her mother, Kristina Heth, encourages her to "think outside the box" and "color outside the lines."